Praise for
Losing Jon

"*Losing Jon* takes you on a journey for truth that will have you questioning everything from start to finish. Broken trust with the police that have sworn to protect you, the unimaginable grief of a mother, and the strength of a community that wants answers. David Parrish provides a daring examination of a tragedy that changed a community forever."
—**Gregg Olsen,** #1 *New York Times* bestselling author

"The twists read like a page-turning thriller, but *Losing Jon* is all fact. This is true crime at the highest level. Scary, heartbreaking, and completely insightful. See why the best stories are sometimes the real stories."
—**Brad Meltzer,** #1 *New York Times* bestselling author

"As both an author and lover of true crime, I found David's book really captivating. He writes from an interesting perspective as the former little league coach of a young man whose life is forever changed after what can only be described as a brief teenage run-in with the law in Columbia, Maryland. David is ultimately drawn into the mix when he learns of the teen's death, ruled a suicide by local police yet clearly anything but. I particularly enjoyed David's folksy writing style, and I found myself thoroughly drawn in by the picture he paints of this small, close-knit community located just one hour from Washington, D.C. *Losing Jon* is a true page-turner, filled with almost too-unbelievable-to-be-true details of one community's fight to find justice for one of its own. Although the story takes place years ago, the issues raised, particularly when it comes to questions of police brutality and cover-ups, are very much relevant today."
—**Lisa Pulitzer,** *New York Times* bestselling author

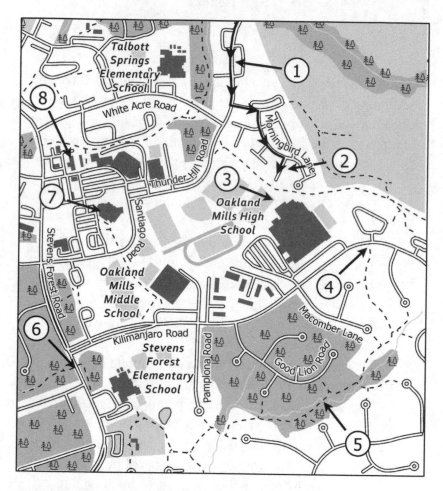

1. Last few turns in Jon's walk home.
2. Vicinity of the parking lot in front of Jon's home.
3. Location of the backstop.
4. Bike path through woods to the bridge and tunnel.
5. Bridge where Jeff Phipps said he woke up.
6. Tunnel where Mama said someone hid.
7. Interfaith center where Lisa House said she was followed.
8. The Other Barn where police and community members met.

Losing Jon

**A TEEN'S TRAGIC DEATH,
A POLICE COVER-UP,
A COMMUNITY'S FIGHT
FOR JUSTICE**

DAVID PARRISH

CITADEL PRESS
Kensington Publishing Corp.
www.kensingtonbooks.com

CITADEL PRESS BOOKS are published by

Kensington Publishing Corp.
119 West 40th Street
New York, NY 10018

All Kensington titles, imprints, and distributed lines are available at special quantity discounts for bulk purchases for sales promotions, premiums, fund-raising, educational, or institutional use.

Special book excerpts or customized printings can also be created to fit specific needs. For details, write or phone the office of the Kensington sales manager: Kensington Publishing Corp., 119 West 40th Street, New York, NY 10018, attn: Sales Department; phone 1-800-221-2647.

ISBN-13: 978-0-8065-4046-7
ISBN-10: 0-8065-4046-X

First Citadel trade paperback printing: May 2020

10 9 8 7 6 5 4 3 2 1

Printed in the United States of America

Electronic edition:

ISBN-13: 978-0-8065-4047-4 (e-book)
ISBN-10: 0-8065-4047-8 (e-book)

To the Bowie-Keyser family: Jim, Sandra, Carlen, and Mickey. No one in a time of grief should have to endure what they did.

To the many relatives, friends, and neighbors who instinctively did whatever they could to support them.

And to Jon.

Losing
Jon

Chapter One

KIDS DON'T THINK. That's just the way it is. A kid who is partying thinks the whole world is partying.

They weren't really kids anymore. All were college students but one, mostly freshmen and sophomores, but they were still kids to me. Some attended college locally and others were home for winter break. There were fifteen of them—eight girls and seven guys. They had grown up together and were all friends or familiar acquaintances.

The tallest in the group, a kid named Chris, was six-foot-two, blond, and a good first baseman on recreational-league baseball teams I had coached against. Jon and Mickey Bowie were identical twins with sandy hair, dark eyebrows, and a frequent glint of devilment in their eyes. They had often played on teams I coached from the time they were eleven until they graduated from high school.

As a group, they had talked for weeks about renting a motel room. Most were under the legal drinking age in Maryland, and those who drank wouldn't have to drive or worry about getting hassled by their parents or the police. Cramming fifteen young people in a motel room without disturbing other guests wouldn't be easy, but kids don't think.

At 11:39 p.m. on Friday, January 5, 1990, a young woman who was the night clerk at the Red Roof Inn on Route 1 just outside of

Columbia, Maryland, placed a call to the Howard County Police Department.

"Howard County Police. May I help you?"

The night clerk identified herself and explained, "A guest just called and said there was a party or something going on in one of the rooms. I'm the only person on duty right now, and I didn't want to go out there."

"Well, I mean, are there narcotics involved? I mean, what—"

"I have no idea."

"Is it a bad party? A good party?"

"He just said there was a bunch of noise."

She gave him the address and phone number.

"You know, it's good to be able to describe to me what's going on because I don't like to send police into situations—"

"Noise complaint."

"Okay, I'll send somebody over."

Several police officers were eating chicken at a chain restaurant practically across Route 1 from the motel, and two of them responded almost immediately. Soon, a half dozen additional police cars would arrive at the motel, followed by one or two patrol cars from the state police barracks a mile up the road.

Things were about to get ugly.

I was coaching a team of ten- and eleven-year-olds the first year that my son Dan, who was ten, and the Bowie twins, who were eleven, played on the same team. The Bowies were the kind of kids that other kids wanted to be like. They enjoyed themselves, were good at what they did, and when the game was over they did something else. Jon was the closest to a genuine free spirit I'd ever encountered. Mickey usually had less to say and was fierier, more physical. Although their personalities differed, I still got them confused even after I'd known them for years. In later years, Mickey told me that sometimes he and Jon switched positions for the fun of it, and Mickey played catcher and Jon shortstop. I never caught them at it.

During that first summer I also met their mother, Sandra. She was a single divorced parent and went by her maiden name, which I kept forgetting and like most people I referred to her as Sandra Bowie. Her family and mine weren't what you would call regular friends—we didn't keep up with each other's lives, and we didn't socialize—but something about Sandra and her sons reminded me of family. Sometimes when our sons were younger, Sandra would drop Jon and Mick off at our house for a sleepover and sometimes I would drop my sons Mike and Dan off at her apartment.

As Jon and Mickey grew older, they played baseball and football and tolerated academics, which did not interest them particularly despite their naturally quick minds. When her sons were old enough, Sandra hired them to do occasional jobs at the daycare center she managed.

Jon and Mickey got full scholarships to play baseball for Dickinson State University in Dickinson, North Dakota. Mickey also planned to play football, so he left home two weeks ahead of his brother to attend football practice. By then Sandra had married Jim Keyser, and she and Jim drove Jon up to Dickinson two weeks later. They planned to make a vacation of it and tour the area after the boys were settled. When they arrived, Jon and Mick informed them that they had decided that North Dakota was not for them. It was too cold, too far from home, too whatever.

Jim and Sandra thought the boys were just getting cold feet and told them that they wouldn't abandon their vacation plans. If the boys weren't staying, they would have to find their own way home. Sandra thought that would be the end of it. She and Jim toured the area and Jon and Mickey took a Greyhound bus home. They enrolled at a local community college, began classes there, and Sandra eventually got over it.

That night at the motel, Jon and Mickey were enjoying winter break during their second year of college.

The Red Roof Inn is a three-story economy hotel a mile or so outside Columbia, just east of Interstate 95. It sits along a high grassy embankment paralleling Route 1.

It was January-cold at about 10:30 that Friday night as fifteen warmly dressed young people got out of their cars and gathered in the parking lot. One young woman went into the hotel lobby and came back out exhaling white air and saying you had to be twenty-one to rent a room.

Only Jeff Phipps, short and stocky with reddish-brown hair, was twenty-one. Jeff had been Jon and Mickey's next-door neighbor for several years, had attended college briefly, and now worked in construction. He and the Bowies lived in adjoining town houses, had gone to the same high school, and sometimes hung out together even though Jeff was two years older. Jeff went into the lobby and soon came out waving a room key.

The room was on the first floor facing the parking lot next to the end unit. It was a standard motel room with a double bed, a dresser with a TV on it, and a round table with two chairs.

Jon and Mickey brought a case of beer and one of the young women also brought a case. One kid brought a pipe that he claimed belonged to someone he knew. It was a tobacco pipe, but it could be used to smoke marijuana. Those I spoke with later wouldn't say who brought the pipe, but they insisted that no marijuana was smoked that night. One young woman brought a camera.

Most of the kids found room to cram in on the bed and they chatted as they waited for a popular late-night talk show to come on, starring Arsenio Hall. A couple of guys moved the chairs by the door and sat there. They had been in the room a half hour or so when the phone rang, and Jeff answered it. He hung up saying it was the front desk and they had to keep it down. They tried, and did for a while.

Jeff made a pass at one of the girls. His girlfriend, a slender blonde, got angry and ran crying into the bathroom. Jeff left in a huff and then there were fourteen. Eight girls, six guys.

A few girls went into the bathroom to console Jeff's girlfriend. Mickey didn't know her that well, but he followed the girls in to see if he could help. He couldn't see that he was helping much and was coming out of the bathroom when someone shouted, "Cops."

*   *   *

The police would say later that they were just doing their jobs that night. I eventually pieced together the official statements of the young people in the motel room along with details from conversations I had with several of them, and the following is more like what I believe actually happened.

As Mickey stepped out of the bathroom, two police officers were standing inside the door. One, a muscular white guy in his upper twenties, was big and really tall. Six-foot-seven. The other, a black guy, was pushing thirty. There was immediate confusion. Kids shouted, "Cops," and the officers shouted, "Out of the bathroom." and "Sit. Everybody on the bed."

Mickey found room on the end of the bed and those still in the bathroom came out and squeezed in here and there. Chris, the first baseman, got up from a chair by the door and sat beside Jeff's girlfriend, who was still sniffling. I don't think Puffy, the only black kid in the room, played baseball, but he was a long-time friend of Jon and Mick's and of others in the room. He was standing near the door and took the chair that Chris vacated.

Chong Ko, who was Korean and had a stocky build and neatly trimmed black hair, was already sitting in the other chair near the door. Chong was also a longtime friend of Jon and Mick's. His family owned and operated several successful restaurants and convenience stores in and around Columbia.

Officer Ricky Johnson, the black officer, stayed near the door, which remained propped open. The tall, white officer, Victor Riemer, walked around the bed and checked the bathroom. He began asking for identification, and a few kids pulled out driver's licenses, but not everyone carried identification.

Officer Johnson ordered the person who had rented the room to stand up. The kids said the person who rented the room had left. This seemed to make the officers angry, as if they didn't believe it. Johnson read a statement about the legal consequences of underage drinking. He said no commissioner was on duty that night to sign the necessary paperwork, so anyone who didn't have identification would have to spend the weekend in jail. Some of the girls started crying. Guys looked at the floor.

Jon was sitting on the heating unit behind Johnson.

"Yeah, right," Jon said. "You can't do that just because we don't have IDs."

Johnson turned sharply to face Jon and said, "Shut the fuck up."

Jon looked down at his chest and back up at the officer and said, "You can't do that."

"You got a problem?" Johnson snapped.

Chris, who had known Jon a long time, would tell me later that Jon knew he had gotten himself into something and wished he hadn't. Jon raised both hands and slumped back against the wall, which Chris knew wasn't at all like Jon unless he was nervous.

"Hey, no problem," Jon said. "No problem."

"Let me talk to you outside," Johnson said.

One girl didn't remember later exactly what was said, but she thought Jon was being smart with Johnson, sort of showing off, and Johnson got angry.

Later, this struck me as a critical point in the kids' encounter with the police. Jon had backed away from the confrontation, and things would have turned out completely different if the officer had simply ignored Jon's remark instead of escalating the situation.

Chong Ko snickered, and Riemer shot him a look. "So, you're a smart ass. Stand up."

Chong stood. Jon had also started to stand to go outside and Johnson gave him a shove, and Jon sat back hard on the heating unit. Johnson frisked Chong and stopped his hand at Chong's jacket pocket.

"What's this?"

Chong took out an unopened pint of grain alcohol, set it on the round table among the opened beer cans, and sat back down.

Johnson turned to Jon again and motioned for him to stand up. Jon stood and stepped toward the door; Johnson grabbed his sleeve and jerked him forward, and Jon stumbled.

Chapter Two

So far as Mickey Bowie was concerned, you didn't touch Jon. Jon could take care of himself, but that's how Mickey was, and Johnson had touched Jon twice.

Mickey was off the bed and behind Johnson in a step. Johnson would say later that Mickey grabbed his arm. Mickey would say that he didn't grab Johnson, but he did put a hand on Johnson's arm from behind to get his attention. Johnson turned and glared at Mickey, and Mickey ignored him. Mickey looked at Jon and said, "No. Don't go outside with him."

Johnson looked down at the hand on his arm and said, "Get your hand the fuck off my arm. Don't you know you can't touch a police officer?" Johnson jabbed his nightstick at Mickey's hand, and Mickey pulled his hand away.

"Where are you taking him?" Mickey asked. "Outside, where you can hit him, and nobody can see?"

This seemed to surprise Johnson. "Ain't nobody goin' to get hit," he said. "We're goin' outside to calm him down."

A flash of black passed in front of Mickey's face. The nightstick pressed hard against his Adam's apple, choking him. Riemer, who was almost a foot taller than Mickey, lifted him up and back. The nightstick shut off Mickey's air supply and he grabbed hard at both ends and pulled forward, trying to get the stick away from his throat. As he and Riemer stumbled about, Johnson jumped forward excitedly and struck Mickey hard in the eye with his own nightstick. Pain came from everywhere, but Mickey couldn't relax. He had to get air.

Jon was standing half outside the room in the opened doorway. He stepped backward out of the room as Mickey and Riemer stumbled toward him and fell through the door. Riemer released his grip on the nightstick as they fell, and Mickey landed on the sidewalk on his side and rolled onto his back.

Riemer landed on the sidewalk beside Mickey and sprang to his feet. He jumped onto Mickey's stomach, straddling him, and struck him in the eye with his fist.

"Shit," Mickey said. "What are you doing?"

Riemer drew back his fist and Mickey pressed up hard with his chest in an effort to flip Riemer off before Riemer could strike him again. Riemer was too large and too heavy, and he hardly budged.

"You're under arrest," Riemer shouted.

Mickey immediately went limp. Riemer rolled him over and cuffed his hands behind his back, and Mickey lay still, facedown on the sidewalk.

Other officers arrived as Riemer handcuffed Mickey, and they were soon joined by troopers from the nearby state police barracks.

To Mickey, the next blow felt like a forearm. It struck the back of his head and drove his chin into the sidewalk, tearing open the flesh.

"Damn," Mickey said. "Are you nuts?"

More blows followed. More officers arrived. People came out of their rooms to watch.

Mickey turned his face sideways and braced himself. "You're real tough," he said, "beating on a kid in handcuffs." Riemer hit him again and Mickey said, "Come on. Is that the best you can do? Give it your best shot." Riemer hit him again and Mickey laughed. "Tough guy," he said. "Real tough guy. Try again."

Chong watched in astonishment from his seat inside the door.

He said later that Mickey was acting tough because he was getting hit and maybe he didn't want to cry in front of the girls.

Jon was standing beside the door with his back to the brick wall and Johnson shouted, "Back up."

"Where?" Jon said. "I'm as far back as I can get." They stared at each other and Jon said, "How about if I just lie down?"

"Right," Johnson said. "Lie down."

Jon lay next to where Riemer straddled Mickey's back.

"Not there," Johnson shouted.

Jon got up and stepped farther down the sidewalk, out of sight of the kids in the room.

"How about here?"

"Yeah, there," and Jon lay spread-eagled on the sidewalk.

Riemer got off Mickey and ran to the door of the motel room. He shouted to the kids inside, "Put your hands on your heads." Some responded slowly, and Riemer shouted again, "Put your hands on your fucking heads."

Several officers gathered with their backs to the door, blocking the view of most in the room. Chong and Puffy could still see a little because they were sitting near the door. Those on the bed could not see outside.

Mickey looked up at Riemer standing near the door. "What did I do?" he asked. Riemer came over and gave him a light kick, nothing particularly sharp, and said, "Shut up."

Mickey was angry and he started shouting, "Get their badge numbers. Get their badge numbers."

Jon raised up on one arm and shouted at Johnson, "Y'all aren't smart enough to catch rapists and murderers, so you just break up parties and beat people up. Y'all can't do this just because you have badges."

An officer Jon didn't recognize reached down with his nightstick and swept Jon's arm out from under him and he fell back to the sidewalk.

"Shut up," the officer said.

Jon raised his head and said, "But y'all can't do this. I'm telling you that you can't do this."

Johnson leaned down and struck Jon in the mouth with his nightstick, and blood began seeping through his lips. Jon winced and shut his eyes. Johnson said, "If you say one more word you'll be arrested, too."

Jon raised his head and pulled his hands together behind his back.

"Arrest me, then."

Neither Puffy nor Chong saw Johnson hit Jon in the mouth. Puffy was not referring to that but to the entire scene playing out before him when he looked across the doorway at Chong and asked, "Did you see that?"

"Yeah, I saw it," Chong said, "and it's real. This is no movie."

Mickey was still shouting, "Get their badge numbers," and Chong called out through the uniformed backs of the officers blocking the doorway, "Mickey, shut up. You're just making it worse."

One of the officers with his back to the door turned abruptly, stepped into the room, and shot the tip of his nightstick at Chong's face. Chong opened his mouth in surprise as the officer came toward him and crammed the nightstick deep into his mouth. The officer told investigators later that the timing was unfortunate, that Chong leaned forward just as he pointed the nightstick. The way the officer told it, maybe the tip touched Chong's mouth. The officer shouted, "Shut the hell up." He jerked the nightstick away and left the room.

Officer Pete Wright was standing near the outside wall. Jon recognized him as an officer who moonlighted in the evenings as a security guard at the Oakland Mills Village Center, which was in Jon's neighborhood.

"Hey, I recognize you," Jon said. Jon would tell investigators later that he didn't actually know Wright. He was just glad to see a familiar face.

Wright walked toward him and said, "Shut up." He stepped around Jon and pressed his nightstick hard against Jon's neck. In an effort to breathe, Jon twisted his head until the nightstick pushed his face straight into the sidewalk.

Officer Johnson was watching Wright, and Mickey called out to him, "If you didn't have that badge and gun, I'd fuck you up."

Officer Riemer came over to Mickey and, with his boot, twisted the side of Mickey's face into the sidewalk as if he was putting out a cigarette. Mickey braced himself as the sharp surface of the sidewalk cut into his cheek and head.

"Tough guys," he muttered. "Real tough guys."

A few minutes later, Riemer lifted Mickey by an arm and wrist and led him still handcuffed through a brick passageway to the rear parking lot.

"What did I do?" Mickey asked again.

Riemer said, "Shut up," and slammed Mickey face-forward into the brick wall. Mickey instinctively lifted his head to protect the bridge of his nose, and the bricks struck his mouth and lower nose, cutting him above his upper lip.

Several officers stood talking in the rear parking lot near a half dozen black police cars with emergency lights off. As Riemer walked Mickey toward the vehicle, two officers came over to assist. One opened a rear door, and Mickey bent over to get in. As if on cue, the other officer pushed him hard in the back. The top of Mickey's head struck the molding above the door, and Riemer and the other officers laughed. Mickey stood up and looked at the officer who had pushed him. "You motherfucker. Why did you do that?"

The officers laughed as Riemer bent Mickey over again. One of the officers pushed him again, and the top of his head struck the door a second time.

Mickey stood and slowly straightened his back. He looked at the officers as if he was about to speak. As they waited, still chuckling, Mickey dropped quickly backward onto the seat. He jerked his feet into the car and turned to face the front before the officers could assist him further.

Riemer leaned across Mickey to fetch a loose end of the seat belt. As he pulled the belt across Mickey's lap, he elbowed Mickey in the mouth, splitting his lip.

"Damn," Mickey said. "Why did you do that?"

"Sorry," Riemer said, laughing. "It was an accident."

Officer Tim Burns, a fiercely muscular man with reddish-blond hair, escorted Jon to a patrol car behind the motel. As Burns led Jon through the passageway, Riemer met them. He brushed against Jon and stared down at him. "You want some, too?"

Jon ignored him, and Officer Burns nudged him forward.

"Go ahead," Burns said. "Keep moving."

While Jon and Mickey sat handcuffed in the back of the police cars, an officer told the others in the room that they could lower their hands. Several officers searched under the bed and in the dresser drawers and began gathering names. Some referred to Chong with mocking terms such as "Ching Ching" and "Boing Boing," and "Ping Pong." A girl asked if any citation against her could be sent to her college address rather than to her home. An officer laughed and said he would make a point of sending a letter to her home.

Officer Riemer came back in the room and joined in the searching and name taking. He found the pipe hidden between the mattress and box spring and asked whose it was. No one responded and he put the pipe in a sack. He took out a small pad and pencil and as he asked for names, his hands shook noticeably.

When Chris produced his driver's license, Riemer said, "I think I recognize you. I attended a party at your house. Right?"

"Yeah," Chris said. Sometimes Chris had parties at his house, especially when his parents weren't home, and sometimes people brought people he didn't know. Riemer was several years older than Chris, but he was single, and at the time Chris hadn't seen it as remarkable that Riemer was attending a party at his house. On that night at the motel, though, Chris didn't want to get into a conversation with Riemer because, as Chris told me later, Riemer looked "pos-i-tiv-e-ly crazed."

"Your driver's license says you were born in seventy," Riemer said. "We can change that to sixty-eight and charge you as an adult."

Chris forgot his determination not to speak and said, "You can't do that."

Riemer laughed and handed back the license. "Shut the fuck up."

No one was charged with underage drinking. The officers finally told those in the room they could leave. Chris was feeling a little drunk and he didn't want to drive, but he wanted even less to mention it.

Chong and Puffy and one of the girls stood around talking for a few minutes in the parking lot, waiting to see what would happen to Jon and Mick. An officer called out from the room, "Hey, you." Chong pointed to himself and the officer said, "Yeah, you," and motioned Chong back into the room.

Later, Chong would say that the officers singled him out because he wasn't afraid of them and they didn't like that. Chong went back inside and sat in a chair by the door. Jeff's girlfriend was sitting in the other chair, and several officers stood around her. She pointed at Chong and said, "Yeah. It was him. He brought the pipe in."

"What are you talking about?" Chong said.

"Stop denying it," she said. "You know you did it," and she started crying.

"She's crazy," Chong said. "Did you guys make her say that?"

Riemer strip-searched Chong in the bathroom and told him he was under arrest.

"For what?"

"You'll find out at the station."

Mickey had waited in the police car for forty-five minutes. The handcuffs were tight and his wrists hurt. As Riemer pulled out of the parking lot, Mickey asked if the handcuffs could be loosened or moved.

"We'll be at the station soon," Riemer said.

Mickey asked again why he had been arrested.

"If you don't shut up, I'll charge you with this," Riemer said, holding up the sack so Mickey could see the pipe.

"You can't do that."

"Haven't you heard of possession of drug paraphernalia?" Riemer asked.

"Yeah, I've heard of it. If you charge me with it, I don't suppose there's anything I can do about it, but it's not mine."

The Howard County Police Department is in a modern, flat-topped, one-story redbrick building a few miles north of Columbia in Ellicott City, the county seat. It's a fifteen-minute ride from the Red Roof Inn. At the station Jon and Mickey and Chong were fingerprinted. They argued and asked what was going on. Officers laughed. Chong protested that the pipe wasn't his.

"Listen," Riemer told him. "You're lucky we like you, or you'd look like your two buddies."

Jon's girlfriend, Jennifer Hollywood, was one of the people at the motel. Jon told Officer Riemer that he wanted to call Jennifer's dad and have him come for them.

Riemer looked at his notes. "I think we'll call your parents."

"Don't do that," Jon said. "My mom'll just get all upset. It's my phone call. Let me decide who I call."

Riemer laughed and picked up the phone.

Chapter Three

WHEN THE PHONE RANG at around midnight, Sandra was upstairs trying to sleep. Jon and Mickey always called to let her know when they would be out late, and they hadn't called.

She had called the parents of practically all of Jon and Mick's friends to find out why her sons weren't home yet, and she was certain they would be angry at her for making the calls. She worried that she was overly protective. She worried that she had given up calling too soon and was not protective enough. She worried that she wasn't a good enough parent. She worried that they might be hurt, and if they weren't then she would give them what for. She rolled over and fumbled on the dresser for the receiver.

The caller was Sylvia Phipps, Jeff's mother and Sandra's next-door neighbor.

"Now don't get upset," Sylvia said in a shrill, excited voice, "but Jon and Mick have been arrested for assault and battery of a police officer."

"What?" Sandra jerked onto an elbow.

"Jeff's girlfriend told me. A police officer brought her here."

Sylvia hung up and as Sandra searched for Jim, she was angry and confused. If her sons had done something they shouldn't have, they should be in jail.

She found Jim half-awake in a recliner in the basement, watching an instructional videotape on golf, and she gave him an agitated account of Sylvia's call.

"Calm down," Jim said. "We don't know the whole story yet. Jeff's girlfriend told Sylvia something and Sylvia told you. That's thirdhand at best."

Then Sandra was angry at Jim. "I'm calling the police department right now."

"Wait an hour," Jim said. "If the boys haven't come home by then or if we haven't heard anything, then call."

"Oh, you just want to finish watching your tape."

"No, if you want to call now then call now, and we'll go up there if we need to. I'm just saying we should wait an hour."

The phone rang at around one o'clock, and Sandra answered.

"This is Officer Riemer of the Howard County Police Department. Your sons have just been arrested for assaulting a police officer."

"I know," Sandra said.

"How do you know?"

"A neighbor told me. I've been waiting to hear from the police."

"Oh," Riemer said. "Well, Jon's here and he wants to talk to you."

After a pause Jon said, "Mom?"

"Are you all right?" Sandra asked.

"No, I'm not all right, and Mickey's really upset. You can probably hear him yelling in the background." Sandra switched her attention, but she couldn't hear Mickey.

"We've both been beat up really bad," Jon said. "My mouth is all ripped up inside. Somebody needs to look at it."

Riemer yelled, "Get him back in his cell. He's out of control," and he was on the phone again.

"Mrs. Keyser," he said, "I can assure you that your boys don't have a scratch on them, and they do not need medical attention. All they need is an alcohol and drug abuse program."

"I'm coming down there."

"Don't do that," Riemer said. "They won't be released for at least six hours, and you can't see them. All you can do is sit and wait."

"If it's going to be six hours, then okay, but I want to be called immediately when they are released and I'll come get them."

"They're big boys," Riemer said. "They can walk home," and he hung up.

Sandra was a petite woman with sharply outlined features. She would say in her native West Virginia twang that she had large ears and her nose was bent a little to one side. She had dark brown eyes and long auburn hair that she usually wore straight down her back or in a loosely tied bun. She was inclined toward tight blue jeans, men's shirts, and dangling earrings, and had the kind of figure that made other women look to see where their husbands were looking.

Sandra met her first husband, Carl Bowie, at Shepherd College in Shepherdstown, West Virginia. Carl had been a star baseball pitcher and football quarterback at his high school in Pisgah, Maryland, and he played baseball at Shepherd. The Yankees expressed an interest in him, but that didn't work out. Neither did their marriage, which lasted only long enough for Sandra to deliver her daughter Carlen and, three years later, Jon and Mickey.

After the divorce, Sandra and her children moved in with Sandra's parents in the two-story redbrick home where she grew up, along a forested, mountainside road just outside of Wardensville, West Virginia. Sandra's degree was in elementary education. She had hoped to find a teaching job after college, but there were few teaching jobs available in the sparsely populated area where she lived.

By the time Sandra finally found a teaching position in Burtonsville, Maryland, a few miles south of Columbia, Carlen was a pre-teen and, very much like her mother, knew her own mind. Carlen was a daddy's girl, and when her father remarried, she voluntarily moved in with Carl and his new wife. Carl and Sandra had little use for each other, but Carlen visited Sandra every few weeks, and every few weeks Jon and Mickey visited their dad and their grandparents.

Sandra stayed hardly a year in Burtonsville. One afternoon an older teacher admonished her because Jon and Mickey had what the older teacher thought were too many black friends, and Sandra laughed. She finished out the school year, but Burtonsville was not where she wanted to raise her sons. She found a job as an assistant kindergarten teacher in Columbia. She rented an apartment in the Stevens Forest neighborhood and soon discovered that to qualify for a more formal teaching job in Maryland she would have to take too many additional college courses. Instead, she took a class at the local community college to earn a necessary certificate for a better kindergarten position. The class teacher recommended her for her next position as director of a daycare center for preschoolers.

In February 1983, Sandra came down with a sore throat and a headache and slept away two days. On the morning that she reemerged into the world, the town was covered by an unpredicted snowfall of more than three feet. Front doors were completely covered by drifts. People shoveled their roofs so they wouldn't collapse. When she came downstairs, Jon and Mick said they couldn't find her car. Sandra thought her car had been stolen, but when she realized it had snowed, she went outside with a broom.

Jim Keyser, tall, lanky, athletic, and brown-haired, delivered the mail on Sandra's route. Jim was also divorced. To please his first wife, Jim had joined her church, driven the church bus, taught a Sunday school class, and almost completely given up beer. Then his wife ran off with a beer truck driver and he gave up church and started spending his Sundays playing golf.

Jim had stayed over with a fellow mail carrier in the apartment complex where Sandra lived. Most of Sandra's neighbors were outside digging out cars and shoveling sidewalks, and Jim and his friend joined in. They saw Sandra stumbling about in the snow, stabbing her broom at cars and occasionally bursting into tears, and they offered to help. Sandra accepted and Jim took the broom and began sweeping off cars asking, "Is it this one? This one?"

Jim finally found Sandra's car and Sandra, apologizing for her cold, went back inside and watched from her third-story window. When they came to the door with the car key, Sandra invited them in for coffee. Jim said that he had noticed her and he admired how she and her sons seemed to enjoy themselves. He asked if she was married, and when she said she wasn't he asked if he could call her sometime.

They were married in August 1986. What tipped the scales in Sandra's mind was how respectful and accepting Jim was of her children. When Carlen visited and Jim came over, he treated Carlen like family. Jim bought Carlen an old, rusted Toyota and spent hours sanding and painting it. Carlen said she'd always wanted a gold car, so Jim painted the Toyota gold. Carlen named the Toyota Fred. Jim wondered at how Carlen and Sandra made such a big deal of the way he had fixed up the car. It was just something that he could do, so he had done it.

Jim had his concerns before the wedding. Sandra was college educated and smart and pretty. He didn't want to go away to never-never land and wake up one morning and find that he had only dreamed it. Sandra liked him, though. She had told him, and he thought he saw it sometimes in her eyes. She had said a bit awkwardly that she loved him, too, and he had gathered himself when he thought it had to be done and said it to her, and that was also important, he supposed.

Jim sold his house in the nearby town of Elkridge and they bought a red-and-tan-brick town house a short walk from the apartment complex where they had met. Their unit was one of nine in a row of town houses that faced a mirroring row of town houses across a short, wide asphalt parking lot. A row of tall ornamental evergreens separated the parking lot from several athletic fields behind Oakland Mills High School.

*   *   *

Sandra paced, talked with Jim about it, and then went to bed. She drifted in and out of sleep throughout the night, wondering what her sons had gotten themselves into. At 6:00 a.m. she was sitting on the side of the bed looking out the window when Puffy's older brother dropped the boys off. She went downstairs and met them at the door.

"Oh my," she said. "What kind of party did you go to?"

Mickey's eyes were swollen nearly shut. One cheek bulged away from his face. Crusted blood on his chin looked like dried dressing on ground hamburger. Both of Jon's eyes were black, his lips were swollen, and bright red blood filled the cracks between his teeth. Jon and Mick both looked angry. They brushed aside her question and went upstairs to shower and fall into bed.

Sandra fretted about the house all day Saturday. From time to time she looked in on her sons as they slept. Had they had weapons of some sort? The thought was preposterous, but why else did they look the way they did unless the police had to take weapons from them?

When Jon and Mickey came downstairs around five o'clock, Sandra was making spaghetti in the kitchen. Her sons were sullen and seemed angry with her.

"Tell me what happened?" she asked, but they wouldn't talk. They sat at the kitchen table staring at her and looking at each other.

"Are you angry at me?" she asked.

"Of course we're angry at you," Jon said. "What kind of mother tells the police that her sons are big boys and they can walk home? They took me back in the cell and I told Mickey, and Mickey was as mad as I was."

"I couldn't believe it," Mickey said.

"I didn't say that," Sandra said. "That's what that policeman, that Officer Riemer, said to me."

The air gradually cleared between them, and Jon and Mickey told her what had happened.

"Did you have guns?"

"What?" Mickey asked.

"You know, weapons of some kind?"

"Are you kidding? Nothing, Mom. It was like we said."

"You believe us, Mom?" Jon said. "You do believe us?"

Sandra didn't know what to think. Why would a police officer play such a nasty trick as to tell her sons she had said something he had said himself? Why did her sons' faces look the way they did unless they had to be stopped from doing something really awful?

Sandra went to the table to look closely at Jon's mouth. He winced and leaned back as she pulled his lip down as gently as she could. Pieces of torn-away flesh dangled inside his mouth.

"This is going to need stitches," she said.

"They can't stitch inside your mouth," Jon said. "Can they?"

"You have to have it looked at," Sandra said.

"I don't want anybody looking at it except Jennifer's mom," Jon said. "She's a nurse. I trust her."

Sandra looked at Mickey's face. "You and I are going to the doctor's office on Monday."

"Mom," Mickey whined.

Sandra found her Polaroid camera and took the boys into the backyard and took pictures of their faces. Jon and Mickey called a friend who came over with a 35mm camera and took more pictures. Jon called Jennifer, whose mother, Claudia, was a nurse at the local hospital. Claudia was working the late shift and wouldn't be home and awake until Sunday.

On Sunday, Jon drove to Jennifer's. Jennifer's mother looked at Jon's mouth and said, "This is serious. You have to go to the emergency room and get stitches."

Jennifer went with Jon to Howard County General Hospital. When a nurse called for Jon, Jennifer went into the examination room with him.

The nurse, Yvonne Last, was an attractive, slightly plump

black woman in her late twenties. She asked Jon, "Who did this to you?"

"Ricky Johnson," Jon said.

"Oh, I know him," Last said. "I've dated him. He's bad news. He likes to act like a bad ass, beating up on people and then bragging to me. You know."

Jon said, "Tell me about it."

Chapter Four

DURING THE PAST YEAR AND A HALF I had fallen out of touch with Jon and Mickey. The last I had heard, they got full scholarships to play baseball for a college in North Dakota. In January, I was at the town mall and I ran into a kid I had coached. We had a friendly chat, and he asked if I had heard that the Bowies had given up their scholarships and come back to Columbia. I was caught so off guard that I struggled for excuses, forgot my errands, and returned home. I found the Bowies' phone number on an old roster and called, and Jon answered.

"Hey, Mick," I said.

Jon laughed. "Nah, Coach. This is Jon. You want to talk to Mick?"

Once I knew I was talking to Jon, I thought I could distinguish his slightly higher, slightly clearer voice. Still, I was irritated and a little embarrassed that I had mixed them up again.

"Not particularly," I said. "I mean, either one. I just called to find out what's going on."

"You mean about school?"

"Yeah. What's the story?"

I don't recall Jon ever hesitating for an answer, and he didn't this time, either.

"It's too cold in North Dakota."

I did hesitate. "Were the books giving you trouble?"

"Nah, that wasn't it. Like I said, it was just cold."

"What about Mickey? Was he having trouble?"

"Nah. They told him he probably would make the football team, and I'm pretty sure I was going to make the baseball team. We just talked about it and decided to come home."

Jon and I talked for several minutes, and I became begrudgingly convinced that he was comfortable with the decision.

"I don't suppose your mother took it too well."

He laughed. "She'll get over it."

"So, everything's going all right then?"

"Well, almost. Mick and I got beat up by some cops over the holidays."

I couldn't imagine Jon and Mick being beaten up by anyone.

"How? What did you do?"

"Nothing," he said. "Seriously. I mean, we had a party at a motel and there was some beer, but the cops just got crazy and started hitting us."

"Did you hit them back?"

"Nah. I'm not stupid. You can't hit a cop. I would have liked to, but they had badges, you know. One of them was pretty big, but I think we could have taken them in a fair fight."

This wasn't sinking in. I paced back and forth in the kitchen, searching for an appropriate response.

"Did you get hurt?"

"Yeah, some. Mickey's face was all cut up and bruised, and he got black eyes. They hit me with a billy club a couple of times and cut my mouth and stuff."

I was at a loss. This was completely outside my frame of reference.

"We can't have that," I finally said. "Is there anything you can do about it?"

"We've got attorneys and filed complaints. The police department is investigating it."

"Well, good. We just can't have that sort of thing." Then I changed the subject. "How's Mickey doing?"

"To tell you the truth, I'm not sure. He doesn't seem to have his head together. He just lays around and hangs out."

"Well, you know Mick. He'll sort things out and he'll be all right."

"I guess. I don't see how there's anything I can do about it, regardless."

"Well, tell him I said hello."

"Okay, Coach."

"And you're sure everything's all right?"

"Sure, Coach. I'm sure."

We said good-byes and hung up.

I didn't forget what Jon told me about the motel incident, but I did assume it would be taken care of. Eventually, I would think of this as the last conversation I would ever have with Jon Bowie.

During the week following the motel incident, Jon read a feature article in a local paper about the Reverend Doctor John Wright, the head of the county chapter of the NAACP. Wright, the article said, had a reputation for taking on local agencies, including the police, and for a willingness to help anyone, race aside. Jon figured that maybe Reverend Wright knew how to go about filing complaints against the police, and he wrote the reverend a letter. He looked up the address of Wright's church in the phone book and drove to the address on a rural road south of Columbia to deliver the letter himself. Wright wasn't there and he left the letter in the church door. When he checked the next day and the letter was still in the door, he put a stamp on it and left it in the mailbox of a home across the street.

Jon's determination made Sandra doubt her own doubts. Still, she wasn't certain that her sons were justified in filing complaints against the police. She knew that people could get excited and see what they wanted to see. She neither encouraged nor discouraged Jon and Mickey, and she kept expecting the issue to somehow go away.

Reverend Wright called Jon and told him it didn't matter that

Jon and Mickey were white. The NAACP was interested in hearing their story. They met with Wright and he recommended an attorney, Jo Glasco, who was a member of his congregation and
had an office in Columbia.

Sandra reluctantly agreed to go along with Reverend Wright's
suggestions, but she said the boys would have to pay for the attorney themselves. She thought this would end the matter, but the
boys began saving money. They met with Glasco, who advised
that, for legal reasons, the boys should have separate attorneys,
and she recommended someone to represent Jon.

With the attorneys' guidance, both boys filed complaints at the
police department against Officers Victor Riemer, Ricky Johnson,
and Pete Wright. This would lead to an internal police department
investigation about whether the officers had used excessive force
or violated any other police department policies or procedures.

The boys also filed assault charges at the courthouse against
the officers. These charges put the case in the normal judicial
process and would lead, they thought, to a day in court when they
could tell their stories to a judge.

The police department, meanwhile, charged Jon and Mickey
with various offenses such as assault on an officer, hindering an
officer in the performance of his duties, and resisting arrest.
These charges were expected to lead to trials in which Jon and
Mickey would be defendants.

In early February, the head of the county police department's
Internal Affairs Division, Sergeant Nelson Graham, interviewed
Jon and Mickey and most of the other kids who had been at the
motel. The Internal Affairs Division, or IAD, was the part of the
police department that investigated complaints against police officers. Jon and Mickey told Sandra that the interviews went all
right, although Officer Graham kept trying to get them to say
they had drunk more beer than they did, and that they were ring
leaders in the group.

Reverend Wright suggested that the boys contact the FBI because that agency investigated complaints against police officers.

Sandra took off work one afternoon and went with the boys to the local FBI office. She waited in the reception area with each son as an agent interviewed the other for well over an hour.

Jon or Mick mentioned that one young woman had taken a few photographs at the motel before the police arrived, and they had copies. The photographs showed nothing unusual—no beer cans scattered about or glassy-eyed people. Just young people smiling at the camera. After the interviews, the agent told Sandra he wanted to see the photographs. He came by their home a few days later to collect them.

A few weeks later, the agent and his boss came to the house. Sandra immediately sensed bad vibrations and noticed that the younger agent wouldn't look her in the eyes. She led the two men into the kitchen and called the boys.

"Mrs. Keyser," the older agent began, "we've looked into this matter, and our investigation shows that there was no wrongdoing on the part of the police officers." Sandra stared at him without responding, and after an uncomfortable silence he continued. "You have to understand, Mrs. Keyser, that police officers have bad days, too."

Sandra was furious, and she remained silent as she tried to control her emotions. She thought, *I work with children all day. If I had a bad day and hit one of them, I'd be out of a job. What kind of explanation is that?*

When she sensed that the blood in her face was cooling, she said, "What else can we do?"

"If I were you, I'd just drop it," the older agent said.

"You don't believe us?" Mickey asked.

The older agent stood as if he had been about to leave, and said to Mickey, "Young man, you should understand that you have to listen to what a cop says. You have to learn to respect authority."

Mickey went, "Pffft," with his lips and waved an arm in the agent's direction.

"Forget it."

Sandra saw the disappointment behind her son's nonchalance.

She saw it in Jon's face, too. As calmly as she could manage, she said, "Why don't you give the boys a lie detector test? Then make up your minds what happened."

The older agent gave Sandra an icy stare and said, "It is our experience that habitual liars can pass a lie detector test."

The lid nearly blew off Sandra's calm, but she had to save the situation for the sake of her sons. Trying to keep her voice from trembling, she said, "What do you think the chances are that there were fourteen habitual liars in the same motel room?"

Sandra still wasn't convinced her sons were doing the right thing by pursuing their complaints against the police officers, but the meeting in her kitchen with the FBI agents was a turning point for her. Regardless of the merits of the case, she didn't think they had taken the matter seriously.

When the FBI agents had left, Sandra went back into the kitchen thinking that she knew a bit about what it felt like to be a black person in America.

"Do you believe us?" Jon asked.

"Yeah," Sandra said slowly.

Mickey looked at Jon. "I still don't think she believes us, but she's in."

Toward spring, Chong Ko was tried in the Howard County District Court for possession of drug paraphernalia at the motel. On the Monday after the motel incident, Chong visited a doctor and got a drug test, which came back negative as he had known it would. He didn't know what that Officer Riemer was thinking by charging him with possession of a pipe that wasn't his, and he didn't know why Jeff's girlfriend had said he had brought the pipe into the room. What he told anyone who would listen was that his family didn't come to America to be treated like this.

Chong had told Officer Riemer that first night at the police station that he was going to get the drug test, and Riemer started calling him at home, first asking for the results of the drug test and then, after the test came back negative, saying that he might be able to get the charge dropped. Chong said, "Sure."

Jon and Mick told Reverend Wright about Chong, who met with Wright. Reverend Wright told Chong that it was outrageous for Officer Riemer to call him at home and offer to drop the charges, that Riemer was interfering with the courts, and that was illegal.

Riemer kept calling Chong, saying that he had arranged for Chong to meet with the Howard County state's attorney, which is what the county prosecutor is called in Maryland. Chong refused at first, but before his court date he met with the state's attorney. Chong didn't speak perfect English, he wasn't familiar with all the legal terminology, and he didn't fully understand all that was said at the meeting—there was something about him doing his part.

In court, Chong told the judge that Officer Riemer had called him at home, and the judge said a police officer wouldn't do that. The judge asked the state's attorney if he had test results on the pipe, and the state's attorney told the judge the test results were not back yet. The judge put the case on the "stet" docket, which meant it was set aside and would be dismissed if Chong stayed out of trouble for a year.

One evening in March, Mick was getting ready to go to a party at the apartment of Chong's older sister. She was out of town and said Chong could use her place. Jon was getting over strep throat and he didn't think he would go. Mickey reminded him that they would be watching what promised to be an exciting game in the NCAA basketball tournament on TV, and Jon decided to go.

As many as three dozen people were there that night. They wandered in and out of rooms watching television and talking. The doorbell rang around ten o'clock and somebody said the police were at the door.

"I'm not putting up with any more of this," Chong said, and he answered the knock. He stepped outside, closing the door behind him, and Jon and Mickey stood on the other side of the door watching through the peephole. It was Officer Riemer and another officer. Riemer wanted to know how many people were in the house, and Chong said he didn't know. Riemer said everyone had to leave, and Chong said, "Fine, but you're not coming inside. I've had enough of you guys."

Riemer asked, "Are the Bowie twins here?"

"They might be," Chong said, "and they might not. I'll tell everyone to leave, but you're not coming in."

When Jon and Mickey heard Officer Riemer ask for them, they ran through the apartment and out the back door. Others were also leaving through the front and rear doors, and Riemer called out for the other officer to go around back and look for twins and hold them, because he wanted to talk to them.

Jon and Mickey ran through the woods, and several others ran with them. They stopped on a hill in the woods and watched as the officers came around back, shining their flashlights on the back of the building and into the woods. Jon and Mickey's cars were parked at the apartment, and they weren't sure what to do. Someone said that since the officers were looking for twins, Jon and Mickey should split up. Then the officers wouldn't know if they were twins even if they saw one of them. A friend walked with Mickey the several miles back to Mickey's house.

Mickey had been home about a half hour when Jon arrived and came into the kitchen. Jon said he and Chris, the first baseman, went to a friend's home in a nearby apartment complex. The three of them were standing outside the friend's door when Officer Riemer drove up in his police car. Riemer looked over at them and then went inside another building across the parking lot. It scared Jon that Officer Riemer asked for him at the party and then showed up where they'd gone after the party broke up.

The next day, Sandra called Sergeant Graham of the Internal Affairs Division and told him she wanted Riemer to stay away from her sons. Graham said Riemer couldn't have been at that apartment complex because it was not in his patrol area. Sandra said, "That's ridiculous. Police cars have wheels the same as any other car. If Jon says Riemer was there, then he was there. I'm telling you that I want him kept away from my sons."

Several days later the FBI agent who had interviewed them came by to return the photographs, and Sandra told him about the party.

"It sounds like Riemer is feeling guilty about something," he said.

"I don't care what it sounds like," Sandra said. "My sons have told the police department and the FBI what happened at that motel, and nobody believes them. Now this guy Riemer shows up at a party looking for them, and then shows up where Jon went after the party. I tell the police and they don't care. I tell you about it and you just shrug it off. What does it take to get you people to pay attention?"

Chapter Five

In mid-April, Sandra, Jon, Mickey, and several others from the motel incident went to the Howard County district court in Ellicott City. The courthouse is a one-story, redbrick building very similar to the nearby police station. Jon and Mickey were to be tried for assaulting a police officer, among other charges. Sandra and the others arrived early and were waiting in the lobby when Sergeant Graham of Internal Affairs arrived. The sergeant shook Jon's hand and said, "You and I need to talk."

They stepped a few feet away, and Sandra listened to their conversation.

"I've got a problem with what you had to say about Officer Wright," Graham said.

"What kind of problem?"

"Are you sure he was the one who stuck the nightstick against your neck?"

"Yeah, I'm sure," Jon said. "I know him from the village center. It was him."

When they finished talking Jon rejoined his mother, and Sandra asked, "What was that about?"

"I don't know," Jon said. "I think he wants me to drop the charges against Pete Wright. I'm not sure what to do."

From what Jon and Mickey had told her, Sandra didn't think

Officer Wright had been the main culprit at the motel, and she told Jon that if the police department wanted to protect Wright, then going along might help in some way.

"I don't like it," Jon said. "I know what happened."

The courtroom resembled a small chapel with its white walls, high, narrow windows, and light oak pews. As Sandra and the others filed in, another case was still under way. They didn't want to disturb the proceedings so they sat in the last two rows.

Sandra's hair was gathered in a ponytail and, from the rear, she would have looked like one of the young girls in the group. A big, tall police officer came into the courtroom. He noticed the large group of young people and went to the front and spoke in whispers to the county attorneys. He returned to the rear of the room and stood behind Sandra with his back to the wall. Sandra had never seen this big, extremely tall officer before, and she paid no particular attention to him.

After a minute she felt a thump against the seat behind her. She ignored it and kept looking forward. Then there was another thump, and another. Keys jangled behind her. She heard a low, guttural growl. After several minutes of this, the officer pushed himself away from the wall and walked up the aisle toward the front. As he passed the group he looked over at Jon and grinned. He continued on to the front, sat in the row behind the county attorneys, and leaned over and whispered with them again.

Puffy was sitting in the end seat in front of Mickey. He turned around and whispered to the others behind him, "Did you see that?"

"Yeah, I saw it," Jon whispered excitedly.

Sandra leaned forward across the seat back. Jon's face was turned slightly away and tears swelled in his eyes.

"Who is that?" she asked.

"Don't you know?" someone asked. "That's Riemer."

"So what?" Mickey said. "He's nothing."

"Like hell. That man's dangerous."

Sandra studied the large man sitting with the county attorneys, and in that moment, her nagging doubts disappeared. She thought, *These kids really are telling the truth.*

The case in progress dragged on. Riemer came to the back again and leaned against the wall behind Sandra and the others. He thumped the back of the seat several times with his knee, jangled his keys, and made low, growling noises. Sandra and the others stared intently forward. After a few minutes Riemer pushed himself away from the wall and started again for the front. As he passed by, he bumped Mickey's shoulder. Puffy was sitting with one arm propped on the end of the seat, and Riemer swept out a hand and knocked Puffy's arm off the seat.

Sandra was up and moving before Puffy had recovered.

"Excuse me. Excuse me," she whispered as she made her way to the center aisle. She found Attorney Jo Glasco and Jon's attorney outside the courtroom in the large waiting room, and she hurried up to them.

"Somebody has to do something," she said. "That idiot is terrifying those kids. Somebody has to do something or"—she took a breath—"somebody has to."

"You go back inside," Jo said. "We'll talk to Sergeant Graham."

Soon after Sandra returned to her seat, Sergeant Graham came into the courtroom, went to the front, and motioned for Riemer to come out with him. After several minutes Riemer came back inside. He turned inside the door, walked along the rear wall, and stopped immediately behind Sandra. He leaned against the wall and jangled his keys loudly.

Sandra jumped to her feet, excused her way to the far end of the row again, and went around the row to the rear wall. She stopped beside Riemer and turned, facing the front of the room. Her intention was to stand beside him as long as he stood there. She was not going to put up with his attempts to intimidate them.

As Sandra stood beside Riemer, she was struck with how tall he was. Her head hardly came up to his chest. Riemer stood with his arms folded across his chest, looking intently forward himself. Sandra folded her arms across her chest, mimicking his position. Her legs began to shake, and her heart pounded. She was afraid she might faint. From the corner of her eye she saw Riemer slowly turn his head and look down at her. She sensed that he wanted her to look back at him, and she kept looking forward.

Jo Glasco and Jon's attorney came into the room, and Sergeant Graham followed them. Riemer looked over at the sergeant and jerked away from the wall. He hurried to the front and sat down, and Sandra returned to her seat.

The court clerk announced the case against Jon and Mickey, and attorneys made their way to the front. That almost took longer than the case itself. An assistant state's attorney, a dark-haired man in a navy suit, said the county was not prepared to go forward. Sandra's sense of it was that the county attorneys were surprised that so many of the young people who had been at the motel showed up to testify.

Jo Glasco objected that she wished to proceed. She said there was reason to believe that the safety of some of the young people was at risk. The judge, a thin, gray-haired man with wire-rimmed glasses, brushed that aside and postponed the trial.

Sandra and the young people grumbled to each other as they left the courtroom. Sandra, Jon, and Mickey waited in the lobby for others to catch up, and Sergeant Graham came out of the courtroom and waited with them. Riemer walked past, crouched down into a slumped posture, ducked his chin down close to his chest, and held his palm sideways to his face like a blinder on a horse's bridle.

Graham muttered, "What a wise ass."

Sergeant Graham had already interviewed many of those who had been at the motel, including Jon. A few days after the case was continued, Graham had Jon return to the police station for a second interview. They talked for a while and then Graham turned on the tape recorder. I never learned why Graham wanted Jon to drop the charges against Officer Wright, but the transcript of that recorded interview clearly shows that Graham had already orchestrated the outcome before turning on the recorder. He then intentionally manipulated Jon's painstaking honesty.

"Okay," Graham said, "after we had some discussion, you said there is a chance that Wright may not have been the person that put the nightstick against your neck."

"Right," Jon said.

"Okay, and can you tell me what you base that on?"

"Okay, 'cause when I was laying on the ground and I looked up, and I told Officer Wright that I knew him, and that I knew where he worked, he walked over to me in a loop where his face got out of my sight. But I saw his feet walk around. And then an officer—it could have been another officer—put a nightstick to my neck."

"Okay. When Pete . . ." Graham paused and corrected himself. "When Officer Wright walked around you, how long was it before another officer approached you and put the nightstick against your neck?"

"It was right as he got right next to me and stopped."

"Could you see the officer's face?"

"No, I couldn't. I could see his hand, and the outside was pressing down with his nightstick."

"He was actually pushing your neck with the barrel of the nightstick?"

"Yeah."

"You said you were laying on the ground outside the motel room, facing toward Washington. Right?"

"Yeah."

"Where was Officer Wright when you saw him?"

"He was standing next to the door. I told him I recognized him from the village center."

"And what did he say?"

"Told me to shut up."

"And then someone, some officer, came up, placed a night-stick—"

"Yeah."

"And you assumed it was Wright in the beginning because he had been the one standing between you—"

"Yeah, 'cause he stopped right next to me and I assumed it was him."

"Okay. So, you're really not sure if Wright was the one who put the nightstick up against your neck?"

"Yeah. Since I looked away, I guess not."

"The only thing that you said when you were lying on the ground was looking up at Officer Wright saying, 'I know you from Oakland Mills'?"

"Yeah."

"You did that because you didn't want him to do anything to you and you wanted him to know that you knew who he was?"

"Yeah. It was like, 'Good, at least I know somebody here.'"

Following this interview, charges against Officer Wright were dropped.

Chapter Six

ONE DAY IN APRIL, out of the blue, Jon said to a friend, "I don't think I'm going to live much longer."

This startled the friend, who asked, "Why would you say that?"

"Call it a feeling," Jon said. "I think it has something to do with a car. Maybe I'm going to die in a car wreck."

Jon began telling Sandra and others that Riemer was following him. John Hollywood, Jennifer's father, said, "Why would a cop do that?"

School, Jon decided, was not to his liking, and he dropped out of the local community college. He thought he might try to find work at the nearby Baltimore-Washington International airport. He was still working from eight in the morning until six in the evening at the daycare center, and he began changing his schedule to arrive at unpredictable times. Sometimes he arrived as early as six-thirty in the morning. One morning he gave Anne Beck, Sandra's middle-aged blond assistant, a license number he had written down. He told Anne the number was for a brown pickup that had been following him, and had followed him again that morning. "It's Riemer," Jon said. "Riemer's following me." Anne gave the license number to Sandra, and Sandra stored it away.

Sandra called Internal Affairs again and told Sergeant Graham she wanted to talk to the chief of police. She wanted Riemer to stay away from Jon. Graham made a note of the phone call and filed it.

Mickey cleaned the daycare center in the evenings, sometimes after nine o'clock. He began seeing two men hanging around the Dumpster. He never got a good look at them, but they were hanging around often enough that it worried him, and he wouldn't dump the trash when they were there.

At two in the morning on Monday, April 30, four months after the incident at the Red Roof Inn, Jon came into Jim and Sandra's bedroom and shook his mother awake.

"Riemer's in the backyard," Jon whispered excitedly. "Come see."

Sandra followed him across the hall to his bedroom. Henry, their curly-haired black terrier, ran in front of them, barking and darting about. Henry jumped at the windowsill and Sandra whispered loudly, "Henry, hush." As she approached the window, she was certain she heard someone running. She looked out onto the tiny backyard below and couldn't see anyone. The gate to their five-foot-high privacy fence was always kept closed. On this night the gate was open.

On Wednesday, May 2, Jon woke Sandra again between two and three in the morning.

"He's out there, Mom."

Sandra followed Jon into the bedroom again and looked out the window into the backyard. She couldn't see anyone, and this time she didn't hear anything. She did notice, however, that the screen to Jon's second-story window had been cut and pushed inward.

On Thursday, May 3, around six in the morning, Jon went into Mickey's bedroom and woke him.

"Riemer's in the backyard," Jon told Mickey.

"Riemer's not in the backyard," Mickey grumbled. "It's just your imagination. Go back to sleep."

Later that morning, Jon drove his silver Mercury Topaz to the daycare center. He made sandwiches for the children's lunch. He joked about with several of them, making them laugh. Then he left work early and spent the better part of the day helping two brothers he knew and their family move to a house a few blocks from where he lived.

Around five-thirty in the afternoon Jon's girlfriend, Jennifer Hollywood, called from Florida where she was attending college. Jennifer was an attractive, athletic blonde, and no doubt the reason John Hollywood coached girls' softball for several years. She and Jon had dated on and off for four years, and now the relationship was serious. They exchanged small talk on the phone. Jon and several friends were planning a trip to the University of Delaware that weekend to cheer for a friend who was the football quarterback. Jennifer described a movie she had seen. She said later that Jon was in a good mood. He told her that Vernon Gray on the County Council was helping him get a restraining order against Riemer, and he wouldn't have to worry about that anymore.

After Sandra came home from work, Jeff Phipps came over several times from next door. Each time, he asked Jon if he was going to a bar called Chicago's later that evening. Each time, Jon said no.

Sandra went up to her bedroom while Jon was in the shower. She heard the water turn off, and soon after the phone rang. Jon had taken a portable phone into the bathroom with him, and he came out with a towel around his waist and the phone to his ear.

"What?" he shouted so loudly that it startled Sandra. She stepped to her bedroom door just as he entered his bedroom. "Fuck that!" he shouted, slamming the door behind him.

This was not the way Jon usually talked around the house. Sandra sat on the side of her bed, slowly brushing her hair as she wondered about the call. A few minutes later, Jon came into her bedroom. He was dressed in stone-washed blue jeans and a dark blue polo shirt that belonged to Mickey. He had been exercising for weeks so he would feel confident in swimming trunks when Jennifer got home from college, and his jeans were loose at the waist. He fidgeted with his belt, tightening it until his jeans wrinkled beneath it.

"Is this too tight?"

"A little," Sandra answered. "Maybe a notch less."

"I feel like my pants are falling down," Jon said in the semi-gruff way he had of laughing at himself. He loosened the belt a notch and lay down across the end of the bed.

Sandra had been a mother too long to jump straight into a subject that concerned her. She continued brushing her hair for a while before asking with casual disinterest, "Who was on the phone?"

"Forget it, Mom."

The tone of Jon's voice said it was a closed subject. Sandra laid down the brush and sat cross-legged on the bed, facing Jon. He headed her off with a new subject. "If I buy Jennifer a diamond, should I charge it on VISA or take out a loan?"

They discussed it and Sandra agreed to cosign a loan if Jon needed it. Jon got up from the bed and hitched his jeans again.

"I'm off to Keith's."

As Jon started out of the bedroom, Sandra said, "Seriously, Jon. Who was on the phone?"

Jon ignored her, and she followed him down the stairs to the front door. "Jon Bowie, you tell me what that phone call was about."

Jon turned and with a calm certainty that chilled her said, "Look, Mom, all I'm going to say is that Monday I'm dropping the charges against those police officers. Now, drop it."

"I won't drop it," Sandra said. "I'm calling the police department first thing in the morning. I'm going to find out what's going on."

"Don't call them, Mom," he pleaded. "Every time you talk to them, things just get worse."

"Well, I am going to call them. I intend to find out what's happening."

"At least wait until Monday," he said.

"All right," Sandra said. "Monday. I'm going to have some answers by then or I'm calling the police."

Jon turned to leave and Sandra reached out and touched his arm. He turned halfway around, and his eyes danced again with their usual confidence. "It'll be fine, Mom. Trust me."

As Sandra closed the door behind him, her mind went somewhere else. Call it a premonition. She saw two men standing in darkness at the rear of a car, putting something in the trunk. Sandra strained to see more clearly until, aloud in her mind, she said, *Oh no. It's Jon. They're putting Jon in the trunk.*

Sandra jerked open the door and ran out onto the stoop and across the tiny front yard into the parking lot, but Jon's car was already out of sight.

Not much would be learned about Jon's activities after he left home that Thursday night. He stopped by the nearby home of his longtime high school friend Keith, and they rode together to join several others at the home of another friend named Scott who lived with his parents a mile away in an adjoining neighborhood.

Later, when the police seemed intent on demonstrating that this was just another beer drinking party, one young woman called everyone who had been there to learn how much each person had to drink that night. She did the necessary math and decided that Jon could have drunk four beers at most. The police also emphasized a beer drinking game that was supposedly played.

Several of those who gathered at Scott's were going later to a nightclub called Chicago's in College Park. Chicago's had a dress code and someone had not dressed accordingly, so they decided instead to go to another bar called The Cellar. Four of them left together a little before ten o'clock. Jon had indicated earlier that he might go, but he changed his mind.

As the others were leaving, Jon and Keith went outside. Jon told Keith that he'd been drinking and he didn't want to drive, and he gave Keith his keys. Keith either laid the keys on another car and the car pulled away, or threw the keys at the car, trying to get the attention of those leaving. Either way, Jon's keys got lost. Somebody ran the car down, and the guys in the car came back and helped search for Jon's keys. Some of those still in the house also came out to join the search. One young woman said later that she helped until it started raining hard and she went back inside. Jon's keys weren't found.

It was not terribly chilly and Jon started walking home. Keith offered to drive him but Jon said he'd rather walk, and he left his car at Scott's. A woman who lived in the end unit, a few doors down from Jim and Sandra, passed him walking down the street a little after ten as she was driving home. Soon after, she took the babysitter home and on the return trip she saw Jon a second time, rounding the last corner onto the street where he lived. The police tried later to get the woman to modify her statement to say that Jon was swinging his arms angrily as he walked, but she refused. She said he was just walking.

Chapter Seven

SANDRA PACED THE HOUSE, went back and forth in and out of the kitchen, checked the wall clock, sat at the table by the window a while, got up and paced again.

For as long as she could remember, Sandra had seen what she thought of as people on her eyelids. When she was younger, she thought everyone saw them. After repeated blank stares, jeers, and scolding in response to her "overactive imagination," she began to keep the things she saw to herself.

Sandra had been born in a Catholic hospital "under the veil," "en caul," meaning that a portion of the placenta still lay across her face. Some people believed this was a sign of special destiny or good luck, or supernatural abilities. There was a story in Sandra's family that when the nuns first saw her, they crossed themselves.

As Sandra grew older, she still saw people on her eyelids, but by and large she ignored them. Sometimes she knew something that couldn't be explained, but she kept such things to herself unless she slipped up.

A friend who was dating a married man once told her that the man was going to leave his wife and marry her as soon as he found a way to tell his wife. Before she thought to catch herself, Sandra blurted, "Don't waste your time with him. His wife is pregnant and he'll never leave her." Sandra didn't know the man or his wife, and she didn't know how she knew the woman was pregnant. The words just came out of her mouth. When the friend asked how Sandra knew, Sandra scrambled for an explanation and finally said she had heard it somewhere. The friend met the man that weekend, and he broke the news to her.

During Jon and Mickey's freshman year in high school, the family was watching the Super Bowl. Jon pulled for one team and Mickey pulled for the other. When Mickey's team scored a touchdown, Jon took a playful swipe at Mickey and missed. He struck his hand against the edge of the coffee table and writhed on the floor in pain. The next morning, Sandra took him to the doctor and an X-ray showed that the hand was broken. The doctor put a cast on Jon's hand and said he wouldn't be starting baseball practice in the spring, and he definitely wouldn't be catching that year.

When they got home, Jon was distraught at the possibility of not playing baseball. Sandra told him to rub his hand gently and to picture tiny butterflies and angels flying around the bone, repairing the fracture with magic thread. She didn't know where the idea came from, but Jon spent hours each day alone in his room, rubbing his hand.

Two weeks later, the doctor took a second X-ray and couldn't find the fracture. He accused Sandra of bringing Mickey instead of Jon. He didn't say how Mickey could have removed the cast from Jon's hand and put it on his own. The doctor removed the cast, but when they got home Jon couldn't squeeze his hand into a fist, and he was worried. Sandra heard the words, and as she heard them, she repeated them to Jon.

"Drink milk. Hold your hand in cold water. When you take it out, squeeze a rubber ball one hundred times. Then put your hand back in the water and start all over."

Jon followed the instructions, and in the spring he was ready when baseball practice started.

Because of such things, Sandra believed that someone might

actually try to put Jon in the trunk of a car. By ten-thirty Jim still wasn't home from bowling and Sandra tried to call Keith, but a message said the phone had been temporarily disconnected. Then she went upstairs to get ready for bed.

Her bedroom window was slightly opened for air, and she heard someone outside call out what sounded like "Jeff," and then "Mickey." There were shuffling noises, and then a car door slammed.

The voice sounded like Mickey's. She went across the hall to Mickey's bedroom, knocked on the door, and opened it. Mickey was lying on his bed with a textbook and he looked up, startled.

"What?"

"I thought I heard you outside," Sandra said.

"Mom," Mickey said, complaining at the interruption. "It was probably Jon. It's almost ten-thirty."

Sandra went to her bedroom and looked out the window. She saw nothing unusual and she went back to Mickey's bedroom.

"There's nobody out there. What do you suppose that was?"

"Well, if you thought it was me, then it probably was Jon. Maybe somebody picked him up to go somewhere. Quit worrying."

Sandra returned to her bedroom and looked out over the parking lot again. No one was there. She put on her pajamas, knelt at her bedroom window, and peered out. Now and then a car turned in and parked. Jim arrived in his silver and burgundy van that he kept so spotlessly clean. He came inside and she heard him knocking about in the kitchen. He came upstairs to the bedroom, stopped at the door, and said, "Oh, you're in one of those moods," and went downstairs to the basement to fall asleep in the recliner in front of the television.

Light showers fell intermittently. An occasional breeze blew rain in through the screen. Moisture accumulated in Sandra's hair, matting it against her forehead, and she ignored it. Droplets formed and ran down her face. There was a sudden downpour and she squinted to see through it.

At around one in the morning she realized that her pajamas

were soaking wet. She got another pair from a dresser drawer and went into the bathroom to dry off and change. She came back to the bedroom window and knelt. The rain had stopped and she looked outside, waiting.

On her eyelids, she saw someone leading Jon into the edge of the woods.

Several people would say that Riemer appeared at a restaurant called Clyde's that evening. Clyde's is a popular restaurant in Columbia's town center and, reportedly, Riemer came in Clyde's dressed in uniform even though he was off duty, and he made a loud show of being there.

A female friend dropped off Jeff Phipps, Jon's next-door neighbor, at Oakland Mills High School that night around 2:00 a.m. This saved her a few turns on her way home, so he took the shortcut behind the school through the evergreens and onto the parking lot. Jeff would say later that he didn't see anything out of the ordinary. Jeff's mother, Sylvia, worked the night shift, and she was outdoors chasing after her dog and a sock when Jeff came through the evergreens. She said it was actually a few minutes before 2:00 a.m.

From her upstairs window, Sandra watched as Sylvia greeted Jeff and they entered their town house.

John Sinelli, a former Michigan police officer, lived with his wife in the end unit closest to the street and farthest from the high school, a couple of doors up from Jim and Sandra. Around 2:00 a.m, a phone call woke him. He answered but the caller hung up. The phone rang a second time and he answered it, and the caller hung up again. Sinelli was recovering from knee surgery and had trouble sleeping. The arrangement of the town houses and the location of the trees channeled sounds to the back of his house from the direction of the high school. Around 2:45 a.m. he heard banging and rattling sounds coming from the back of the school. The sounds lasted for ten to fifteen minutes. He came downstairs, looked outside, and didn't see anything. He opened the sliding doors for air, turned on the television, and watched a cable news channel.

Around 3:00 a.m, a dark, late model, full-size car backed up toward his house from farther up the street near a cul-de-sac that overlooked the rear of the high school. The car's parking lights were on, and Sinelli could tell by the shape of the taillights that the car was a Chrysler LeBaron or a similar model. The car pulled away and turned on its lights. Later, the police report suggested that Sinelli might have seen the morning paper carrier's car, but Sinelli insisted that it wasn't. One morning paper carrier drove a station wagon; the other drove a pickup and didn't usually arrive until around 5:00 a.m.

The crack of lightning came only an instant before an explosion of thunder. I sat straight up in bed, wide-eyed and still half asleep.

The thunder rolled and disappeared and I lowered my head back onto the pillow. There was a moment of still silence. Then rain fell straight and hard, as if God had opened a wide door in heaven.

The hard rain lasted only a minute or so. It was followed by another silent pause and then by a light, windless shower. The bedroom window was opened slightly for air, and the pattering of raindrops on the roof and the grass gradually blended with my wife Jane's deep, soft breathing, and then with my own.

I was still a smoker at the time, and the next morning I sat at the round table in our small kitchen smoking a cigarette and pulling on my shoes. Jane was puttering about the kitchen in a flannel nightgown. I asked if she had heard the thunder and the rain, and she hadn't. I said I was amazed it hadn't awakened her.

At least a week had gone by, maybe more, before Jane found the occasion to share her own experience of that night. She said that once she had also sat bolt upright for no apparent reason. It was such an uncharacteristic experience that she sat in the darkness wondering what might be wrong.

We agreed it was odd that each of us had experienced an unordinary awakening well past the middle of that night, of all nights.

Chapter Eight

AT AROUND SIX O'CLOCK on the morning of Friday, May 4, 1990, the body of Carl Jonathan "Jon" Bowie was found hanging from the back of a softball field backstop that stood immediately behind Oakland Mills High School. At that time of year, the sun is not yet up, although the sky was growing increasingly light.

A backstop, for those not versed in baseball terminology, is a tall, chain-link wire fence supported by long pipes. It stands behind home plate to stop foul balls. The better ones have vertical wire sides that angle out and away from the back and a wire roof that inclines upward toward the playing field. This was one of the better ones.

Thirty yards away, a woman jogged along the bike path that paralleled the first baseline, looking over at the backstop. The woman thought at first that she was seeing some sort of effigy. The prom was scheduled for that night, and maybe students had hung something there as a gesture, or a prank. As she abandoned the bike path and approached the backstop from the rear, she saw it was a person, and she was looking at his back. His legs and body from the shoulders down dangled over the back of the backstop, touching the wire. His shoulders pressed against the horizontal pipe that separated the back from the forwardly inclined roof.

She ran around to the front of the backstop. The ground was hard packed and her jogging shoes left no noticeable impressions in the infield dirt, despite the scattered showers a few hours before. She looked up at the young man through the wire. His head was turned to one side with his cheek against the wire, just above a horizontal pipe that supported the roof. The base of his right palm lay on the pipe near his right shoulder. Almost two feet above the pipe, the thumb and fingers of his left hand clutched the wire in a tight grip.

She turned and ran across the first baseline, across the bike path, through a row of tall, evergreen shrubs onto a short, residential parking lot. She had no way of knowing that until the night before Jon Bowie had lived a few doors up on the right in a town house that was empty at the moment except for Mickey, who was upstairs asleep, or that his mother was hardly out of sight on her way to work. The woman knocked on several doors until a slender woman finally answered. The woman didn't want to call the police unless she could be sure they were needed. She walked down to the evergreens, looked through, and hurried back to her house to make the call.

As a second woman walked past the fields on the bike path, she thought someone was doing an odd callisthenic exercise on the backstop. She and others stopped their jogging and early morning walks with their dogs and gathered on the grassy area between the bike path and the backstop. The first woman came back through the evergreens and joined them. A man walked to the backstop, looked up at the body, and said, "My God, he's dead."

The Oakland Mills section of Columbia was in Officer Tim Burns's patrol area, and he was the first law enforcement officer to arrive. Burns was the muscular officer who, at the motel, had led Jon to his car and later had given Jeff Phipps's girlfriend a ride home. Officer Burns also was a close friend and drinking buddy of Officer Riemer. Burns's police cruiser came slowly around the school with blue lights flashing and no siren. He parked at the end of the school parking lot near the backstop and got out of his car. He walked to the backstop and inspected the body from the ground.

More police cars arrived. Several officers, especially those in plain clothes, stayed in the rear of the school. Others went around front to deal with traffic.

The second woman on the scene stood with the crowd on the small, grass-covered slope. She thought what a nice young man the person on the backstop appeared to be. He looked so well-groomed in his stone-washed blue jeans, dark blue polo shirt, and heavy, round-toed boots, with his sandy, nearly blond hair neatly trimmed. She couldn't help thinking that somewhere a mother waited anxiously for him to come home. She also thought that the odd position of the body was ominous, as if it had been intentionally arranged as some sort of warning.

An officer stood beneath the wire overhang and began photographing the body. A red and white rescue truck arrived. First responders took a ladder from the truck and leaned it against the backstop. A plain-clothed detective climbed the ladder and inspected the body. A length of blue vinyl-clad cable a quarter inch in diameter was clamped permanently to the backstop roof, near the upper edge. The cable, pulled tight, continued down the roof where a short end, connected to the upper length by a turnbuckle, was fastened in a tight loop around Jon's neck. The detective tugged at the cable but could not loosen it, and he climbed back down. Uniformed and plain-clothed officers agreed aloud that something had to be done fast. School would open soon and children would be arriving.

Someone finally cut the cable. Then a rescue squad worker climbed the ladder and, leaning out and reaching, looped a thick rope around Jon's stomach and tied the rope in a large knot at the middle of his back. Another rope was draped across the roof to the front of the backstop, and another rescue worker stood on the ground in front of the backstop holding the rope and slowly lowering the body. When Jon's feet were near the ground, rescue workers held the body, removed the rope, and laid the body faceup on the grass behind the backstop.

Onlookers began checking their watches and discussing among themselves whether they should approach the officers and give their names and addresses. Some agreed to do it. Others said they had to leave to get ready for work.

The high school principal had been called at home and she arrived. She looked at the body and said she knew it was one of the Bowie twins but she couldn't be certain which one. The assistant varsity baseball coach joined the group and leaned over.

"It's Jon Bowie," he said, pointing to a small scar that was all but hidden by an eyebrow.

A deputy medical examiner for the county arrived, soon followed by Detective Wendell "Bud" Rudacille, who would lead the investigation of the case. Rudacille was a tall, thin, long-faced man. Together, the detective and deputy medical examiner inspected the body as it lay on the ground. They determined between themselves that the death was a suicide. The detective would insist later that the deputy medical examiner had made the decision.

I feel that I must pause here to inject that, coincidentally, I was acquainted at the time with two of the county's medical examiners, neither of whom was the examiner called to the scene of Jon's death. One was an emergency room nurse, and the daughter of a friend. The other was her husband, a house painter who had been an army medic. Neither was a forensics expert. To become a county medical examiner, you took a course. Both were capable people, but it would have been a stretch to ask either of them to make a scientific ruling of suicide.

Anyway, the school's athletic director arrived. She explained to the police that the cable apparatus had been attached to the backstop several years earlier, and that Jon Bowie had been one of several athletes who helped attach it. Once a year, for field day, the cable was lowered and a tire connected so students could crawl through as one of the events. Sometimes the cable was lowered so baseball pitchers could attach the tire and pitch base-balls through it.

When the cable had first been installed, it was tossed on top of the backstop when it wasn't in use. Parents complained that it was dangerous to have a cable lying loosely on the backstop where it could fall and perhaps be misused. Someone could be injured.

The athletic director had procured a combination lock with a key slot on the back to fasten the loose end of the cable to the backstop roof. She could never remember the combination, so she always used the key to unlock it. The next field day was scheduled for the upcoming week, and she had inspected the cable the week before. If it had not been locked down at that time, she told the officers, she would have noticed. The police searched the grass all around and in a nearby garbage can, but they could not find the lock.

The athletic director had wrapped gray duct tape around the turn-buckle so students crawling through the tire would not scratch themselves. She pointed out the tape to a detective, who inspected it. Half of the tape had been removed, and by the freshness of the exposed adhesive, the detective observed that the tape must have been removed recently. He looked around in the grass for tape fragments, but could not find any.

Jon carried a house key on a red key tag. The key was separate from his car keys, and it was never found, which could well explain how someone entered his home that morning through the front door, three hundred feet away as Jon's body still lay behind the backstop.

Jim and Sandra had left for work, and Mickey was still upstairs asleep. The intruder's noises woke Mickey, who listened as foot-steps came up the stairs and went into Jon's bedroom. The telephone rang and the intruder hurried down the stairs and out of the house. After several rings, Mickey answered the phone in a sleepy voice. It was Sandra.

"Has Jon come home?" Her voice was panicked. "He hasn't come to work yet."

"I heard him come in a few minutes ago," Mickey told his mother. "He came upstairs and went in his bedroom. When the phone started ringing, he ran downstairs and went out. He should be there any minute."

According to official records, at approximately the same time that the intruder would have been leaving the Bowie-Keyser residence, Riemer's attorney got a phone call telling him that Jon's body had been found. Then the attorney called Riemer, to tell him. If this is correct, it essentially rules out the possibility that it was Riemer who broke in that morning because, in an age before cell phones, the attorney called Riemer at home.

Riemer then called the woman with whom he later claimed to have spent the better part of the previous evening. She didn't answer right away and Riemer shouted over the recorded voice of the answering machine, "Pick up the phone. Jon Bowie's dead."

Chapter Nine

WHEN MICKEY BOWIE PLAYED BASEBALL, he had what is called *field sense*. The ball comes hard at you on the ground and you field it. Maybe you glance at third base so the runner there doesn't try for home. Maybe you slow your step a bit so the runner at second base knows you haven't forgotten him. Then, as smoothly as if all you had done was field the ball, you throw out the batter. It would be unusual for a person with such a natural awareness to be caught off guard.

Still, on that morning in May, Mickey was caught off guard. It was almost nine o'clock when he answered a knock at the front door and two tall, plain-clothed men, Detective Rudacille and another detective, showed him their badges.

Rudacille asked, "Are you Mickey Bowie?"

"Yes sir, I am."

"Jon Bowie's brother?"

"Yes sir."

"Well, he's dead."

Mickey said, "Prove it," and Rudacille handed him the fake ID that Jon used to buy beer.

Mickey looked at Jon's picture on the ID and handed it back.

"You'd better call my mom."

He showed them in, gave them the number, and pointed to the

phone on the kitchen wall. Then he quietly sank into a fog of despair that would not begin to lift for many months.

Except for the industrial-grade-glass front door, the daycare center Sandra managed looked like a small, one-story brown barn. At six-thirty Sandra parked and got out of her white, economy-size pickup with the wide red stripe down each side. She unlocked the school door and entered the large front room to begin her day's work. Soon, teachers and group leaders began arriving. They scattered throughout the three large classrooms, opening cabinets, laying out toys and worksheets, and pausing to greet the children who came early.

By eight o'clock when Jon still hadn't arrived, Sandra called home. Mickey assured her that Jon had just left the house and was on his way, but then eight thirty came, and then eight forty-five.

When Anne Beck, Sandra's assistant, arrived a little before nine, Sandra was standing at the reception counter by the front door. Her face was pale and tense, and she gripped the edge of the counter as if she might fall.

"Jon's not here," Sandra said. "He didn't come home last night."

"Quit worrying," Anne said. "He'll be here."

There was a trace of uncertainty in Anne's reassurance. Jon had changed his arrival times frequently for the past few weeks so they couldn't be predicted, but he always told Anne and Sandra beforehand and arrived when he said he would.

Ordinarily, Sandra wouldn't have said it, but it just came out of her mouth.

"They took him in the woods, Anne. He's dead."

Anne looked as if she had been slapped. "Who? What are you talking about?"

"I don't know," Sandra said. "I just know it."

"Shut up," Anne said. "You're talking crazy."

"I mean it, Anne. We're going to get a phone call."

"I'm not listening to this," Anne said, and she stormed away, jerking off her jacket.

The phone rang at nine o'clock and Sandra grabbed it. She stood listening and then, in a voice so intensely calm it all but trembled, said, "Okay," and hung up the phone. She looked at Anne.

"That was the police. They asked me to come home. I don't think I can drive."

Anne drove and Sandra sat in the passenger seat, squeezing her hands together. "The police said there was a little problem," Sandra said, and she laughed a laugh of controlled hysteria. "They said there's nothing to worry about, that I just need to come home." She sat quietly a moment, then added, "They're lying."

"We don't know yet," Anne said. "Just wait."

"He's dead, Anne. I know it. I think they put him in the trunk of a car. His car is parked in somebody's driveway. He's not with his car."

"Stop it," Anne shouted. "I'm not listening to that."

The trip across town normally took fifteen minutes, but Anne made it in closer to ten. The car was still moving when Sandra slung open her door and jumped out. The image that burned itself indelibly into Sandra's future memories was Mickey standing inside the storm door looking out, his shoulders shaking and tears streaming down his face.

Sandra stopped a few steps from the door and said, "No."

Mickey saw her and nodded as if to say, "Yes."

Sandra opened the door and they held each other in a long hug. Mickey's sobbing stopped and he managed, "Don't believe them, Mom. Don't believe them."

The detectives were in the kitchen, and Rudacille asked Sandra to sit down.

Sandra said, "No. Just tell me what you have to say."

"It's about your son. Jon." He waited, as if he wanted her to say something, to help him somehow, but she waited, too. Finally, Rudacille said, "He's dead. He committed suicide."

Sandra stood a moment as if the blow had knocked her out but she had not yet fallen. Then she turned and ran stumbling out of the kitchen into the living room. She fell to her knees and looked down at the carpet. Then she looked up at the ceiling and screamed.

"No!"

When Sandra returned to the kitchen, the color was gone from her face.

"There's no way in hell he killed himself," she said to Rudacille. She spoke through her teeth in as normal a tone as she could manage, but her voice kept getting louder until she was shouting. "If you want to know what happened to him, ask Riemer. He's been harassing Jon for weeks. If Jon's dead, Riemer killed him."

Rudacille's face flashed red and he shouted back, "He hung himself at the school. I was there. I saw him. He was hanging eight feet off the ground. Do you want to come down to the station and see the rope?"

Anne watched, stunned. She asked Rudacille, "Where is the . . . where is Jon?" Rudacille looked at her and didn't answer. "Sandra should identify the body," Anne said.

"It's not necessary," Rudacille said. "We have a positive identification from the teachers. The body is at Slack Funeral Home in Ellicott City."

Sandra went to the phone and called Jim, and he left work immediately to come home. Then she called Attorney Jo Glasco and Jo said she would be right there. Then she phoned Jennifer Hollywood in Florida.

"Who are you calling?" Rudacille asked.

"Jon's girlfriend," Sandra said in a tone that suggested it was none of his business.

"Let me talk with her," Rudacille said.

Sandra broke the news to Jennifer and gave her time to react. Then she handed Rudacille the phone. He asked if she and Jon had argued or if he was depressed. When Rudacille hung up, Sandra shouted at him, "This is no suicide. Somebody's going to have to investigate this, and I can't see that you're investigating anything. You've already made up your mind."

Still red-faced, Rudacille asked where Jon's room was. He went upstairs and Anne followed him. He looked around for a suicide note, but there wasn't one.

Sandra's employer, Barbara Baney, arrived. When Rudacille and Anne returned to the kitchen, Sandra was telling Barbara that Jon was at Slack Funeral Home.

"What about an autopsy?" Barbara asked.

Anne answered her. "Detective Rudacille here says it's not necessary."

Rudacille still was angry. "Listen," he said to Sandra. "This is my investigation and it's no movie. Your son committed suicide, and I'll decide if there's an autopsy."

"We'll see about that," Sandra shouted at him.

Attorney Jo Glasco arrived, followed closely by the Reverend John Wright, a stocky black man whose belly-out, chest-back, chin-in posture made him look taller than his average height and dared anyone to confront him.

"What's this about an autopsy?" he asked in the demanding voice of a man accustomed to ordering mountains to move.

Anne and Barbara and Sandra shouted versions of Rudacille's decision. Rudacille shouted that it wasn't his decision, it was the decision of the county medical examiner. Wright finally held up a hand for the shouting to stop, and when it did, he turned to Rudacille.

"On behalf of the N double-A-C-P, I am insisting that there be an autopsy on this child."

Rudacille started to speak and Wright interrupted him. "Please do not misunderstand me. I am not asking. If you ascertain in your official capacity that there might not be a necessity, then please be advised in the presence of these people that, if necessary, I will pay for it myself."

Barbara Baney called information for the number and then called the funeral home. After a brief conversation Barbara said into the phone, "The family will be requesting an autopsy." Then she hung up. She said to Sandra, "The woman at the funeral home says it's highly unusual not to request an autopsy, even if it might be a suicide."

Sandra flinched. "It's not a suicide."

By midday Detective Rudacille was accompanying Jon Bowie's body from Slack Funeral Home in Ellicott City to the offices of the State Medical Examiner in Baltimore. Neighbors and friends converged on the Bowie-Keyser home throughout the day. Several mentioned a jogger in a white T-shirt. Later in the day Detective Rudacille returned and Sandra told him about the jogger, hoping the man might have seen something that would help the investigation. Rudacille said that he couldn't go looking for every man wearing a white T-shirt. Sandra was already on red alert, concerned that the police were more interested in proving that Riemer had not been involved than investigating, and after Rudacille left she went to the other town house units around the parking lot, asking about the jogger. She found him, living in a unit across the lot, but he didn't know anything that would help the investigation. He had seen the body and abandoned his jogging to return home and call the police.

As visitors came and went, Sandra was desperate for information. A visitor that same afternoon told her that his brother worked at the fire and rescue station that had responded to the call to the backstop; he said that Jon's family needed to see the rescue squad's written report. He didn't say why, but Sandra took it seriously. She called a friend who would know when the rescue station got a call, and the friend called later that afternoon and said the station was likely to be empty.

Sandra drove to the small, redbrick fire and rescue building, parked in front and, finding the front door opened, went inside. A police officer sat at a desk behind the glass window of the reception area, talking on the phone. Sandra waved to him, smiled, and proceeded to a file cabinet with her back in plain view of the officer. She searched the drawers, but several were locked and she found nothing useful. Then she waved and smiled again at the officer, he waved back, and she left.

Nothing came of this excursion, and Sandra never learned why she supposedly needed to see the report, but such determination and daring on the same day she learned of her son's death reveals a bit about why she would soon turn Howard County upside down.

Chapter Ten

IN THE EARLY 1970s, I found myself in the Washington, D.C., area looking for a house. My wife Jane and my two sons, Mike and Dan, who were approaching school age, were still back in Brandon, Mississippi, outside of Jackson, where we had followed my federal public health job from my hometown of Durham, North Carolina.

Jane grew up in a suburb of Youngstown, Ohio. She is a petite strawberry blonde with captivating blue eyes and a cheerful nature: as grounded a person as I've ever known—a genuine ambivert. People linger to converse with her at social gatherings because she is so naturally interested and engaged.

Jane and I met as college students when we both had summer jobs at the same resort hotel on Connecticut's Long Island Sound. She was a waitress and I was a pot-washer. We lived in North Carolina our first few years of marriage and then in Mississippi for three and a half years. We decided that Mississippi was too far from both of our families. I took a lower-level management position with a federal regulatory agency in Washington and drove north alone to start my new job and look for a house.

One hot morning in July, I sat alone in a nondescript hotel room in a Washington suburb, reading a long article in the real estate section of the *Washington Post* about Columbia, Maryland, a planned community some twenty miles up Interstate 95, halfway to Baltimore. The town had been created and made famous by real estate developer James Rouse in the late 1960s, and had the advertised nickname of "New America." In what was reported on my car radio as the thickest smog to cover Washington in twenty-five years, I drove up to check it out. By the time I took the two-lane exit off the interstate the smog had all but disappeared behind me.

There didn't seem to be a straight road or street in the town. I got lost and wandered for miles past lakes and trees and asphalt paths for bicycles. The houses were a little on the underbuilt side and shaded mostly by four-foot-high saplings, but I was looking for something more than a house. Trees grow.

I eventually found myself in the town's central section, which consisted mostly of a large lake, a low-slung motel, a lakeside restaurant, a two-screen movie theater, some recently built office buildings, and a large mall, all in earth tones. Except for the movie theater marquis, there were no billboards or lighted outdoor signs and only the occasional traffic light. I parked across from the movie theater and went into a small exhibit hall. Two or three other people stood with me facing a high wall where we looked up at a fifteen-minute film about this new town. When the town was completed there would be schools in every neighborhood and families of various races and religions living together on the same streets. Twenty percent of the land would remain undeveloped, so there would always be trees and wildlife.

I left the exhibit hall and immediately got lost again. I parked in front of a one-story brick elementary school and, finding the front door unlocked and no one in sight, I went inside for an un-guided tour. I had no way of knowing that this was the school my children ultimately would attend, or that Jon and Mickey Bowie would soon live a short walk away.

I made a down payment on a small, split-level house, parked my car at the home of a newfound friend and coworker, and took a plane back to Mississippi. Jane and I packed our belongings in a rental truck and we moved to New America.

For several years I made the rush-hour commute to Washington, D.C., and worked my way up the bureaucratic ladder at the regulatory agency. The commute and bureaucracy finally became a bit much, and I quit the government job. A friend helped me get into technical writing in the telecommunications industry, and I faked it until I began to get it right. The pay was decent, although companies I worked for kept getting bought out and downsized and I had to find another company that at least temporarily wanted to give permanent jobs to technical writers.

On that morning in May, I drove the thirty miles to Gaithersburg, Maryland, to my second or third permanent technical writing job. Toward five in the afternoon I realized that I needed to stay late to finish some work, and I called Jane to tell her. I was hoping she hadn't prepared a nice dinner and I hadn't forgotten any plans I'd promised to remember. I had just begun explaining that I would have to work late when Jane interrupted.

"I've got terrible news."

There was nothing in Jane's voice that sounded terrible, and I almost kept talking. Instead, since Jane is not one to exaggerate, I stopped myself. She said, "Jon Bowie's dead," and she hardly got it out before bursting into uncontrolled sobbing.

I couldn't respond. I waited to say something, feel something, but I couldn't, and Jane regained control.

"I was going to wait until you got home to tell you."

Words came from somewhere far back in my head, and I could hear them coming out.

"What happened?"

She burst into tears again, controlled herself, and was finally able to say, "He killed himself."

"I'll be right home."

She was crying again as I started to put down the receiver, so I waited.

"David, I'm so sorry," she said.

It was then I realized that she was crying for me. She knew that when I did feel something, it would cut deep.

The thirty-mile drive from Gaithersburg to Columbia took forty-five minutes under the best of conditions. It consisted mainly of back roads that ran north and east a few miles above the nation's capital through little crossroad communities and what remained of farm and horse country. During Friday rush hour the best I could hope for was an hour's drive. From time to time I slammed the steering wheel with the base of my palm and shouted, "God damn it, Jon," and, "You of all people," and, "How could you do something so stupid?"

Jane and I stood in the kitchen and she told me what she knew. She had withheld the part about the backstop until she could tell me in person and, when she told me, it didn't feel right.

"You know," I said, "that doesn't sound like something Jon would do. It's too . . ." I searched for a word and settled for ". . . showy."

I didn't want to go to Jim and Sandra's for all the natural reasons. I didn't know what to say, how to act, to feel. I made excuses to myself such as that I didn't want to intrude. I called a friend of Mickey's and asked what he'd heard. He had been to the house and said lots of people, mostly Jon and Mick's friends, were still hanging around. He thought I should go.

I hadn't been to Sandra's since before she married Jim and our sons were exchanging sleepovers. I didn't know where they lived. The friend gave me directions and we hung up. I told Jane I wouldn't be gone long.

Evening darkness had fallen when I arrived. Cars filled all of the parking spaces facing the buildings, and several cars were double-parked behind them. Young adults and a scattering of older ones filled the center of the parking lot. I drove slowly through the crowd, nodding through the window as a few young people I recognized looked up. I parked at the end of the street facing the evergreens and walked back through the crowd. I grabbed the arms of young people I knew or nodded to them.

Sandra saw me coming. I had usually seen her in summertime, and she was always tanned and vibrant. Now her face was deathly pale and the flesh on her cheeks sagged. She walked toward me saying, "Thank you so much for coming."

I'm normally self-conscious about hugging people other than family, but this was a time to forget such things. We hugged and I said, "I'm sorry." A man I didn't recognize arrived and Sandra turned to greet him.

Jim was standing in the group Sandra had left and I went over. I had spoken to Jim once or twice at baseball games. We shook hands without speaking.

John Hollywood and his wife, Claudia, the parents of Jon's girlfriend, Jennifer, were in the group. As they resumed their conversation, John said that someone had found a .22 caliber bullet at the backstop.

"Two bullets," Claudia said, correcting him. "One was coated with dirt and looked as if it had been there a long time. The other was new."

I asked what it had to do with anything and John interrupted Claudia to answer.

"The police couldn't have inspected the area very well if people are finding bullets after they leave. They're not taking this seriously."

I didn't push the issue. People have a hard time accepting suicide. I waited a respectful time, half listening. When there was a pause in the conversation, I asked Jim where Mickey was, and he pointed to the front door.

"Top of the stairs, door on the right."

Chapter Eleven

THE STAIRS WERE JUST INSIDE the front door. I met two or three young people coming down as I went up, and we acknowledged each other with silent glances and slight nods. The sounds of low voices came through Mickey's bedroom door. I knocked lightly and, although no one answered, the voices stopped and I went in. Mickey sat stretched out on his bed with his head leaning against a propped-up pillow. His eyes were swollen and distant, and his face was expressionless. Several young people sat on the floor or on the foot of the bed. A television was on and no one was watching it. Mickey looked up and a flash of recognition passed across his eyes. I wove my way through the bodies and offered a handshake, and he took it.

"Tough, Mick," I said.

"Yeah. It is that."

I held the grip for a few seconds and released it. The odd thought that crossed my mind was that I wouldn't have to worry about confusing him with Jon anymore. I retreated back through the bodies and stood for a short time with my back against the door. The absence of conversation indicated that the young people would be more comfortable if I left. I raised a palm to Mickey and he raised one back, and I left and closed the door behind me.

Jim, Sandra, John, and Claudia had gathered in the kitchen. The two women sat at the round, antique oak kitchen table by a window, Jim sat in an oak rocker, and John was getting a can of beer from the refrigerator. He lifted one, offering it to me, and I declined with a negative nod.

"I'd better be going," I said.

"Please don't," Sandra said.

The intensity of her plea persuaded me despite my feelings of awkwardness, and I took a seat at the table. John and Claudia and Sandra were animated and angry as they recounted events of the day, and Jim listened quietly, smoking a cigarette.

"They wouldn't let me see him," Sandra was saying. "They took him straight to the funeral home. If Anne Beck and Reverend Wright and Barbara hadn't been here, they wouldn't have done an"—she hesitated and then pushed quickly through—"autopsy."

They talked about the recent suicide of a teenager in a nearby neighborhood. He had shot himself in his bedroom while on the telephone with his girlfriend.

"He left a note," Sandra said. "They did an autopsy and roped off the bedroom and investigated for three weeks before they called it a suicide. They didn't even rope off the area around the backstop. What's different here?"

"I'll tell you what's different," John said.

"I'll tell you what's different," Sandra said, interrupting. "They don't want to investigate it. They're afraid Riemer had something to do with it."

"Hold it," I said. "Who's Riemer?"

For an hour or more they talked excitedly about the Red Roof Inn, about Jon being followed, and about Riemer thumping the bench in the courtroom. Twice, Sandra left the room with tears flooding from her eyes. Each time she returned after a minute or two, dry-eyed and chiming in. After the second trip out of the room she reached on top of the refrigerator where she retrieved a Polaroid photograph and handed it to me. The picture was a shot of Jon and Mick standing side by side. Mick had a black eye, his face was bruised, one cheek was swollen from his eye to his chin, and his chin was raw. Jon's lips were swollen, and one eye was bruised. I remembered my last conversation with Jon when he had said that he and Mick had an encounter with the police, and I had assumed it was taken care of.

"I think I'll have that beer," I said. I handed the photograph back to Sandra, and John Hollywood went to the refrigerator for the beer.

Eventually, a half dozen young people crowded in the kitchen doorway, listening and chiming in. A young woman who had been at the Red Roof Inn said Riemer had a reputation for being a bully, and she related other stories of people he had roughed up or harassed. "Everybody's heard about the kids at Wilde Lake," she said, referring to a high school in western Columbia.

"What about them?" I asked.

"I don't know their names. One was a wrestler. The cops beat up him and his friends. I think Riemer was one of the cops."

I knew someone who had wrestled for Wilde Lake, and I made a mental note of it.

Chong Ko said in excited and heavily accented English, "I saw the police beat up Jon and Mickey. One stuck a billy club in my mouth and we weren't doing nothing. Just having a party. Now Jon is going to testify against the police and he committed suicide? Sure." He shook his head.

Jim got up to answer a knock at the front door. He came back a step behind a trim, middle-aged black woman dressed in a professional, two-piece gray suit and carrying a leather portfolio. Sandra stood and introduced her to me across the table. Her name was Jo Glasco, and she eyed me with suspicion.

"He's all right," Sandra said, but the attorney wasn't convinced. She hugged Sandra and sat to my left at the table. She reached in her portfolio and hesitated as she eyed me again. She pulled out a two- or three-page letter and handed it to Sandra.

"I got this today."

Sandra took it but her eyes didn't focus on it.

"In essence," Glasco said, "it says that we can get a restraining order."

"Against who?" I asked.

Glasco gave me another who-are-you look and Sandra said, "Riemer. To keep him away from Jon." Then she laughed a soft laugh of irony.

"That detective," Sandra said, "that Rudacille kept saying that he knew that Jon had been depressed because Jon had an argument with his girlfriend. It wasn't Jon who had an argument. It was Mickey. Mickey and his girlfriend broke up."

"When did this Rudacille say that?" I asked.

"This morning when he told me about Jon."

"Regardless of whether it was Mickey or Jon, how did he learn it that fast? I thought you said they came here straight from the school."

"I don't know," Sandra said. "It's what he said."

There was an animated discussion about a lock that hadn't been found, and Jo explained that Jon wasn't found hanging from the front of the backstop. He was practically lying on the roof at the rear, holding onto the wire mesh.

"He was what?" It just came out of me.

Glasco repeated it and we sat looking at each other. I had known Jon since he was eleven, and he was one of the most agile kids I had ever coached.

"You mean that this kid committed suicide with the means of his salvation in his hands?" I held my hands in front of me as I said it, clutching the air, trying to feel the wire in my hands, to imagine how a person could have the determination to lie there and die. Sandra winced and left the room.

"That's what they are saying," Glasco answered.

I don't know if I said good-bye. I just know I left. Jon and Mick's friend Chris, the first baseman, was in front of the house and I took his upper arm in a greeting grip.

"You still be here in a half hour or so?"

"Sure," he said. "I guess. What's up?"

"I don't know," I said. "I'm not sure. I mean, nothing. Just asking."

"Yeah, I'll be here."

Jane was in bed when I got home. I went straight to the basement and turned on my computer. I typed and retyped what I gradually realized was a petition. Finally, it read:

Because there is presently under way a legal matter based largely on allegations made by Jon Bowie against a member or members of the Howard County Police Department, we the undersigned citizens of Howard County, ages eighteen or older, believe that there should be an independent investigation by a police agency outside of Howard County into the circumstances surrounding Jon Bowie's death. We make no presumptions about those circumstances and believe that it would be irresponsible to do so prior to a thorough and independent investigation.

I printed twenty-five copies and returned to the Keysers'. Chris was still standing in front of the house. I handed him the petitions and asked if he would pass them around and get them signed. He read the top sheet slowly.

"Sure, Coach," he said.

I explained that he had to keep one copy as a master in case he had to make more copies.

"Okay, Coach."

I told him to give one to each person and let each make copies. He looked at me and made a determined effort at a grin.

"Coach, I got it. Don't worry about it."

I was nearly home when I realized that I hadn't gone inside to mention the petition to Jim or Sandra.

Chapter Twelve

THE DAY AFTER JON'S BODY WAS FOUND, Sandra walked her black terrier, Henry, around the evergreens and along the bike path that passed the backstop thirty yards away. She stopped to look at a heart-shaped wreath someone had stood in front of the backstop, bouquets woven into the wire, and various memorabilia attached or laid on the ground by mourners and well-wishers. Sandra walked to the front of the backstop and took a photograph of the flowers and mementos. Then she continued her walk.

On Monday morning, Jane and I called our offices and said we wouldn't be in. The funeral home was a one-story sandy-brick building that, from a distance, could have been mistaken for the branch office of a bank. Sandra, wearing a black dress and nose-length veil, was obviously dazed as she greeted people in the red carpeted foyer. She introduced me to her brother Jack and said I needed to talk with him. She walked away with Jane, and Jack and I stepped into a side room. Jack was a serious, dark-haired man in his thirties. He introduced himself as an administrator for a college in western Maryland.

"Sandra says I can trust you," he said. "Something's not right about all this."

"How do you mean?"

"At the very least, it appears that the police are determined not to investigate. You heard about the bullets that were found?"

"Yeah, but I can't make anything of it." Where I was raised .22 bullets were almost as common as blackberries. Jack was from West Virginia, so he was likely to have seen a few as well. When I first heard about the bullets, I automatically discounted the dirty one. It could have been lying in the grass for some time. The newer bullet seemed like a detail worth remembering.

"What do you make of it?" I asked.

"If nothing else, the police didn't exactly comb the area."

"Someone could have held a gun on Jon and made him climb the backstop. Somehow they dropped a bullet."

"Why would you think that?"

"No reason," I said. "Just speculating at the possibilities."

"Sandra told you about the tape that she found?"

"What tape?"

"Gray duct tape, in her backyard. Several strips that looked as if they had been torn off of something. The police say that some of the gray duct tape that was wrapped around the cable had been torn off. If it's a coincidence, it's an odd one. Jon thought that Riemer had been in his backyard."

"If the tape came from the cable, why leave it there?" I asked. "That would be stupid."

"Killing somebody is not exactly a sign of higher intelligence," he said. "There was some orange cord, too, like the cord from a lawn edger."

I thought it over. "I'm having a hard time putting a police officer in Jon's backyard."

"Who knows?" Jack said. "If nobody investigates, there's no way to prove he was and no way to prove he wasn't."

"What about the lock?" I asked.

"The what?"

"I heard that the cable was locked down."

"Right."

"If the lock was there and they don't find it, then Jon had to climb the backstop twice. He had to climb up and remove the lock somehow, climb back down and dispose of it in a way that it couldn't be found, and then climb back up and hang himself. It sounds more deliberate than depressed to me. If nothing else, it's a reason not to jump to the conclusion that he committed suicide."

"I'm pretty sure they didn't find it," Jack said. "I doubt that they're looking."

Jack thought that because of the way the cable was arranged, the person who put it around Jon's neck was left-handed. I had trouble following his reasoning and before I could ask more about it, a gray-haired man stuck his head in the door and said it was time for the family to be seated. I studied Jack as they talked, and I decided that he looked like a calm and intelligent person.

Jane was waiting for me in the entrance hall and we started into the funeral parlor. I wouldn't have joined the line to pass by the opened coffin but most of the two hundred card chairs that all but filled the room were already occupied, and I thought we were waiting to be seated. By the time I realized we were in line to pass by the coffin, other people had lined up behind us and it seemed disrespectful not to continue.

As we approached the coffin, I braced myself. The coffin was made of dark, heavily lacquered cherry. The lid was in two parts and the lower part was closed. Jon's hands lay one on the other below his waist. Thirteen—I counted—long-stemmed red roses lay in a fan arrangement on his chest. His high school baseball jacket, orange letters on black, was folded neatly at his far side, displaying his favorite number, thirteen.

Then Jane and I were first in line and I glanced at Jon's pasty face. I paused for a brief, respectful time, moved on, and immediately regretted that I hadn't lingered more.

We found seats off to one side. Sandra sat with Mickey and Carlen and other family members in the front row. I assumed that the blond, muscular man next to Sandra was her first husband, Carl, Jon's father. Jim sat in the second row, behind Sandra, and I wondered at Jim's considerate gesture of relinquishing his seat to Jon's natural father. As I got to know Jim better, I would realize that it was the kind of courtesy he was inclined to extend naturally.

A stocky black minister spoke first. Jane leaned over and whispered that he was Reverend Wright of the local NAACP. Wright talked compassionately about someone named Carl, and I leaned over to Jane and whispered that Carl was Jon's first name. Then attorney Jo Glasco read a psalm about justice and how evil eventually gets its reward. When she finished, a heavy silence filled the room.

A large, white minister with a dark blond mustache that matched his wavy hair spoke next. He got Jon's name right. When I thought he was winding down, he said, "I know that many of you are not convinced that Jon Bowie took his own life, but whether he did or he didn't, it is a serious issue that must be addressed." Then he went on about why any who were in despair should not succumb to such drastic action. I knew that with so many young people present it needed to be said, but it irritated me anyway. I leaned over to Jane and whispered, "There's not a young person in this room who thinks that Jon committed suicide."

The preacher ended by saying, "If Jon Bowie did not commit suicide, we have to stand together, hold hands together, and demand the truth together. Only the truth can set us free."

There's a special feeling that sometimes comes when you walk into your own empty house. There's an underlying order to it, and it's never as cluttered as you thought you left it, or it doesn't matter as much as you thought it did.

Jane and I hung our coats in the closet by the front door and wandered into the kitchen. I tried to explain something about Jon that I couldn't seem to get into the right words.

"He was who he was," I said. "That's a wonderful thing, and not as common as some might think. It's not that I saw him and Mickey that often, but there was a part of me that looked forward to the next time I'd bump into them at the mall or some other place. He was a part of my life that, without necessarily even thinking about it, I always expected to be there."

Then I was crying and shaking as if I would never be able to stop, and Jane held me.

Chapter Thirteen

A SECOND FUNERAL CEREMONY took place two days later in Wardensville, West Virginia. Sandra's parents, John and Ava Aylor, had come to Columbia almost immediately when they learned about Jon's death, and they were usually among the crowds of people in and out of Jim and Sandra's home. John was a retired high school principal in his late sixties and Ava, in addition to being a lifetime homemaker, had been a fire and rescue dispatcher for thirty years.

The detective on a homicide case usually attends an autopsy, but when attorney Jo Glasco mentioned that Detective Rudacille had been present during Jon's autopsy, Sandra was more than skeptical. She was so adamant, in fact, that Rudacille would try to pressure the medical examiner into ruling Jon's death a suicide that her dad decided to pay for a second autopsy.

A large crowd, mostly from Wardensville and Columbia, came to the second funeral ceremony at the local Methodist church. Some of the young people from Columbia arrived in limousines, and neighbors came outside to see what was happening. There weren't enough seats in the church, and the crowd spilled out into the churchyard. Reporters with notepads or followed by camera crews mingled through the churchyard asking for interviews. After the ceremony, a large crowd gathered in the church basement for food and conversation. Sandra's dad paid for a huge spread, and a big part of his intention was to keep people busy until the reporters finally departed.

Later in the afternoon, a much smaller crowd gathered graveside at the small cemetery on a wooded hillside just outside of Wardensville. When the ceremony ended, a hearse drove the body to the office of the regional medical examiner in Morgantown, West Virginia.

Sandra insisted that, instead of returning to Columbia, Mickey should stay in Wardensville with his grandparents. She was convinced that the police had been involved in Jon's death, and she imagined a terrifying scenario in which they had intended to kill both twins—first Jon, making it look as if Mickey had been responsible, and then Mickey, committing a suicide of regret.

Mickey also worried that he had been the intended target. It was Mickey, not Jon, who had broken up with his girlfriend, and Mickey's car, not Jon's, had been parked on the street that night, at the end of the row of town houses.

One night while Jon's body was still in Morgantown, and Mickey was still living in the safety of Wardensville, Mickey had a dream. In the dream, Jon was crying. Mickey asked, "Jon, why are you crying?"

"Everyone thinks I committed suicide," Jon said.

Mickey said, "No one thinks you committed suicide."

Jon stopped crying, and he laughed.

"Good," he said, "because I didn't."

The reporters that showed up in Wardensville continued the whirlwind of television and newspaper stories that followed Jon's death. All seven of the local Baltimore and Washington television news programs carried stories on the morning, noon, and evening broadcasts. Most stations showed shots of the Red Roof Inn and of the backstop decorated with flowers, cardboard signs, and memorabilia. One station showed Officer Riemer taking out his garbage. The television stories didn't go into much detail. They mentioned that the police had charged Jon and Mickey with resisting arrest and assaulting an officer, and that Jon and Mickey had charged the police with using excessive force.

Newspaper articles often gave Jon's name as "Carl," and said that he was twenty instead of nineteen. They usually referred to him as a man, and I began to suspect that the choice of that word was intended to make it seem that the police had been required to deal with serious offenders when taking care of the motel incident. I also noticed that the newspaper articles often were placed on the same page as an article about an officer of the year or a detective who had pulled a cat out of a tree. I eventually would learn after various off-the-record conversations with reporters that news stories can be very dependent on police sources, and reporters can say only so much when their jobs depend on obtaining future information from the police. Regardless, the basic story of Jon's death got out despite the mistakes and insinuations.

The *Baltimore Sun* reported that family and friends did not believe Jon's death was a suicide. John Hollywood was quoted as saying that Jon had no reason to kill himself and that an officer had been harassing him. The article referred to Chong Ko by his American name, Steve—giving his last name as Coe—and saying that he and the twins had been arrested for possession of drug paraphernalia and resisting arrest. The FBI had been asked to intervene, but a spokesman said the bureau was not likely to get involved.

I was reasonably certain that neither Jon nor Mickey used drugs, and neither had been charged with anything involving drugs. And Chong had insisted convincingly that he had been falsely charged. Some mistakes in the articles were clearly accidental, but I began to sense that some were intentionally misleading, with details provided by the police.

The *Washington Post* reported that the county state's attorney had confidence in the local police, but over five hundred people had signed a petition asking for an outside investigation, and he was open to having an outside investigator assigned to his office.

The chief of police, Fred Chaney, said Jon had an 18 percent blood alcohol level at the time he died. A level of 10 percent will get you charged for drunk driving in Maryland.

The *Howard County Times* said that Chief Chaney was moving to dispel rumors that foul play was involved. The autopsy, the article said, showed that Jon died of asphyxiation. Detective Rudacille was cited as saying that the body had not been moved after the death. I didn't know at the time why Rudacille would make a point of saying that, but eventually the photographer who took the official photographs would say off-the-record that a police officer had struck Jon's knees with a flashlight so the body dropped farther off the top of the backstop and hung more from the back. The photographer had photographed both positions. Rudacille didn't mention the photographer, but he did mention that, ironically, Jon had helped to construct the cable apparatus two years earlier as a student. Rudacille also said there were no grass stains or dirt on the clothing or any other signs to indicate a struggle. The story ended by stating that, in the motel incident, Jon had been charged with assault and resisting arrest, and repeated the misinformation that he had also been charged with possession of drug paraphernalia

It struck me as odd as I read the articles that the police were revealing autopsy results, pounding away at charges against Jon and Mickey, and emphasizing such things as drug paraphernalia and Jon helping put the cable on the backstop. It seemed that, instead of conducting an investigation, they were defending a position.

Ginny Thomas, our state delegate to the Maryland House of Delegates, called me at home one evening. Jane and I had known Ginny, a cordially determined brunette in her forties, through mutual friends for a dozen years, and we campaigned for her among our friends. Ginny knew I coached baseball, and she asked if I knew the Bowies. She thought a meeting should be held between the police and people in the community who were concerned about the investigation of Jon's death. She wondered if I would mention the meeting to Sandra's family and try to persuade them to attend.

Ginny was bona fide good people, a grassroots politician who took the job for the simple purpose of providing a service, and she could see that things were getting hot. In one of those little-known stories that didn't make the news, police had tried to break up a group of teenagers having a beer drinking party at the field where Jon had been found. The teenagers refused to leave and threw beer bottles at the police and shouted, "Murderers." In another isolated incident, someone had broken out the headlights of a parked police car. Maybe the police retaliated or maybe it was just routine that they followed on the bumpers of young drivers in the neighborhood until drivers got nervous and made mistakes, and the encounters often ended in shouting matches.

In a flurry of phone calls and short visits after returning from West Virginia, Sandra at first agreed to attend the meeting. She talked with her attorney, however, and changed her mind. Then she decided to go anyway in spite of her attorney's opinion. But she wasn't certain she should attend. It went back and forth, and I finally called Ginny and said we would just have to wait to see if Sandra came.

In preparation for the meeting, I spoke with several of Jon's friends. I also attended a sizable gathering of young people at John and Claudia Hollywood's home. Several of those who came had been interviewed by police regarding Jon's death, and most of them found the interviews unsatisfactory. They were convinced that no real investigation was taking place. Several said they had been shown photographs during their interviews and asked such things as, "Doesn't this look like a suicide to you?" Detective Rudacille, the officer in charge of the investigation, had told one young man during a taped interview that he was convinced Jon had committed suicide.

I compiled a list of concerns and sent the list to Ginny. She forwarded it to the chief of police so there would be ample time to prepare responses. The list contained a number of tough questions about obvious discrepancies. How did the police explain the missing lock? Where had Jon gotten enough beer to have an 18 percent blood alcohol level at six in the morning when he hadn't been home and the stores were closed? Where was he between 10:20 at night and the time he was found? Why were the police insisting on an 11:00 p.m. time of death when someone who had walked past the backstop around 2:00 a.m. insisted he saw no one? Where was Officer Riemer that night? And on and on. We agreed that anyone could attend the meeting, but to keep the proceedings orderly, I would present the list of concerns.

Chapter Fourteen

MY MOTHER CAN SEE THINGS.

Mama's psychic abilities were not a central part of my childhood. It was more like in the Old Testament, where a miracle of some sort happens every hundred years or so. In the telling of it, though, it can seem that they were everyday occurrences. If you pressed Mama about it, she would say she had a gift from God, but she preferred not to talk about it. She didn't want people to think she was crazy.

My parents grew up dirt poor in the heart of tobacco country in North Carolina's pre–World War II Sandhills region. My brothers and I grew up borderline poor ourselves, at first anyway, but I didn't notice. My dad handled money well, and when I was about six, we moved to a forty-eight-acre farm on a dirt road outside of Durham. Aside from cleaning and cooking—which she hated— and helping to keep up the farm, Mama spent her working years wrapping cigarette packs in cellophane on an assembly line in Durham. My dad was a skilled toolmaker in a machine factory.

At times, Mama would be going about her housework and, hardly looking up, she would say so-and-so was dead. Then we would get a phone call from a relative or friend saying they wanted to tell us about so-and-so, and when the funeral would be. At other times she would say, "I wonder who that is?" or, "Oh, it's so-and-so," and then the phone would ring.

When I was twelve, my dad and younger brother were in a bad car accident. Mama looked up at the dining room ceiling and said, "Get cleaned up. Your father's been in a wreck and we need to go to the hospital. The sheriff will call." The sheriff called a few minutes later.

During World War II, my dad was a lineman in France, Germany, and Austria, and then a trained jungle fighter in the Philippines. When the war in the Pacific ended, he wasn't allowed to write to Mama and tell her that he was coming home. In the winter of 1946, he was finally put on a train in New York City along with other soldiers and sent to Fort Bragg in Fayetteville to be discharged from the army.

We were living in Raleigh with an aunt and uncle and, as the family story goes, it snowed uncharacteristically deep for North Carolina that night. Mama didn't want to say anything at first and have my aunt and uncle think she was crazy, but she finally had to say something.

"Terry's in Raleigh," she said. "We have to go to the train station."

After some fuming and complaining, my uncle drove us there. The train had stopped for only an hour or so. The soldiers were allowed to mill about on the wooden platform and stretch their legs, but they weren't allowed to use the phone.

Mama hurried onto the platform with my brother in tow and me in her arms, and she found my dad in the crowd of soldiers. They hugged, and she told him how she had just known he would be there. Then my dad got back on the train with the rest of the soldiers and went to Fort Bragg to be discharged.

I could share other stories about my mother's psychic ability. This is enough though to provide some understanding of why, when I began to suspect that something about Jon Bowie's death wasn't right, I did what seemed natural.

I called Mama.

My parents were retired by then and living in a redbrick cottage on a quiet side-street in Durham. Mama was in her late sixties and her hair had turned white. Mike was away at school, Dan was out with friends, and Jane was at a meeting. I paced between the kitchen and living room for a while. Then I picked up the wall-phone receiver in the kitchen and called my mother.

"I know you don't like to do this," I said, "and I know it's hard when it has to do with family, but there's something I need you to, you know, to look at."

"Don't tell me too much," she said. Her voice was resigned and weary, as if she wasn't feeling all that well and she was accepting only because she knew I hated to ask.

"Somebody I know died. The son of a friend of mine."

"I'm so sorry," she said.

"Thank you. There's something about it that troubles me, and I wondered if you could try to get a sense of it."

"Okay," she said. "Just tell me his name and how old he was. Don't tell me anything else."

"His name is Jon, for Jonathan. It's spelled J-O-N. He's . . . he was nineteen."

"Okay. I don't know how long it will take, but I'll call you one way or the other."

I hung up and went into the basement family room to watch television, but I couldn't concentrate. I turned off the television and paced back and forth for fifteen minutes. Our family room's not large, and I was a bit like a tiger in a cage. The phone rang and I dashed up the short flight of steps and into the kitchen and jerked the receiver from its cradle.

"Tell me," Mama said, and she sounded upset, "what was he hanging from?"

"It was a backstop, the wire thing that stops foul balls behind the batter on a baseball field."

"Is it a tall, fence-like thing?"

"Yes."

"Oh. I didn't know what it was called."

"Mama, did I tell you he was found hanging?"

"He was, wasn't he?"

"Yes, ma'am, he was."

"I wanted to be sure I was seeing the right place. I'll call you back."

She hung up and I went back down to the basement to pace. After ten minutes the phone rang again, and I dashed up the steps to answer it.

"Do they know who killed him?" Mama asked.

"They say it was suicide. They say he did it himself."

"Oh no," she said. "I don't think so. I'll call you back."

I didn't bother returning to the basement. I paced back and forth between the kitchen and the living room. I was near the wall phone when she called again, and I answered the first ring.

"Mama?"

"Yes." I waited a moment and she continued. "This is hard. I'm not sure exactly what it is that I'm seeing, but there's something wrong here. Something terribly, terribly wrong."

"What do you mean?"

"I don't know. It's as much a feeling as anything else, and it scares me. I've never been so frightened. It's . . ." and she searched for a word, ". . . it's evil. It's something very evil. It really scares me."

"What should I do?"

"I don't know. I'm tired. I don't think I can do any more tonight. I'll try again tomorrow."

"Okay, thanks." I gave her more specifics about what I had heard, and I told her how I knew Jim and Sandra and Jon and Mickey.

"David?"

"Yes."

"I don't think this was a suicide."

"An accident maybe?"

"No, I don't think so. It was worse than that. They meant to do it."

"They?"

"I think so. And David?"

"Yes."

"Be careful."

"About what?"

"About . . . everything. I mean it, David. Be careful."

I knew it was difficult for her to separate motherly concern from whatever she had seen, so I tried to get her to clarify.

"Is this Mama talking or is it . . ." I didn't know how to end the question, so I let it dangle.

"I don't know," she said. "I wish I did. Maybe both."

The young people I spoke with at John and Claudia Hollywood's had said they wanted a police officer they knew and trusted to attend the upcoming meeting. They gave me a name. It seemed like a reasonable request, so I took a few hours off from work one afternoon and went to the local police department. It was located a few miles north of Columbia in Ellicott City, an old mill town that served as the county seat and whose main street had evolved toward gift shops and restaurants.

I told the officer behind the glass partition why I had come, and I found his reaction surprisingly cool. He went away without explaining and soon returned with several higher-ranking officers. The one who seemed to be in charge was in his late thirties or early forties and, like me, average in height. The word *smug* comes to mind. I explained my mission and he said, "You suffer from a misconception, Mr. Parrish. There will be no meeting."

I could feel my face turning red from anger and, as calmly as I could manage, I said, "I didn't come to discuss whether there would be a meeting. State Delegate Virginia Thomas tells me that she has already arranged the meeting with the chief of police. Perhaps you were not informed. I came simply to request that someone the young people are comfortable with attend the meeting."

His face reddened slightly, and I decided not to press the point. I gave him the name.

"That gentleman is no longer employed here as an officer," he said.

This surprised me, and I suggested an officer I knew who was also a good umpire. At least I could represent him comfortably to the kids.

"Why him?" the officer wanted to know, so I told him what I was thinking. "He works in my office," he said, "but just because a man is a good umpire doesn't mean he should be doing the other."

"Who would you suggest?"

"I don't think we have to get into that," he said. "We'll decide who represents us at the meeting."

He obviously saw our conversation as a power struggle. I didn't want to jeopardize the meeting by coming away empty-handed, so I tried again.

"If you look at it from their point of view, you can see why the kids would want someone there they know. It seems to me that it gives the meeting a better chance for success. What can we work out?"

"There's nothing to work out," he said. "Now, if you'll excuse me . . ."

He and his entourage turned and left me standing in the lobby.

Dan was at an age when he was often out at dinner, and that night Jane and I ate alone. Even in my own home I'm not that comfortable with out-loud prayers, so I do a short grace and then we eat. We were passing peas and potatoes and I told Jane about the visit to the police station.

"You know," I said, "I don't want to form any hasty opinions, but these boys are starting to piss me off."

Mama called.

"Write this down," she said. "You have to tell it to Sandra."

I found a pencil in the junk drawer in the kitchen and a small pad of paper on the counter. "Okay."

"Tell it to her just like I tell it to you."

"Okay."

"Sandra has to be careful. The person responsible for Jon's death knows that Sandra provides the intensity that keeps the story alive. That puts her in danger."

"Do you mean someone might try to hurt her?"

"Just write," she said. "Yes, that's what I mean. There is a person who knows what happened, maybe who did it, but he would never talk. He has no conscience. I can't see his face, but I can feel his evil. It's very frightening. She must not go back to work. She works, doesn't she?"

"Yes, ma'am. She manages a daycare center."

"It's important that she not go back to work. If something is going to happen to her, that's where it will happen."

"She'll have to go back eventually," I said.

Mama paused. "If she insists, then she has to be watched all the time. Somebody has to follow her to work and somebody has to follow her home. Anytime she's outside there has to be someone with her. All the time. Is there going to be a trial?"

"Mama, there are more trials scheduled than I can keep track of. There's a grand jury getting ready to start, there could be a trial from the charges that Jon and Mickey made against the police officers, and Mickey is supposed to go on trial in June for the charges against him."

"That one," she said. "The one in June. I think it will all come out then."

I looked with disbelief at what I had written.

"Mama, I can't tell Sandra all this. She's in grief, and besides, I don't know her that well. This would be like adding to her trouble. You know better than I do that things you see are not always one hundred percent reliable, or don't always mean what we think they mean."

It wouldn't be accurate to say that my mother never swears or curses, but she seldom does, and it's usually with a self-conscious little giggle. This time she didn't giggle. She exploded.

"Then what the hell do you think I'm doing this for?"

"Okay, I'll tell her."

People still were constantly filing in and out of Jim and Sandra's house, and on Saturday, a week and a day after Jon's death, I didn't want anyone else present. I didn't want to be there at all, but I had promised my mother. When Sandra answered my knock, her face was drawn and pale. I asked her through the screen door if she would mind coming outside, and she went to fetch a windbreaker. We walked a few paces down the sidewalk and I stopped there to ensure that no one overheard me.

"I'm not sure how to go about this," I said. "I really don't want to add to your grief."

I could see that she wasn't inclined to speak.

"My mother has what I guess you could say is some sort of gift. I've been talking to her about Jon, and she says there are things I should tell you."

Sandra still didn't respond. I took my notes out of my pocket and referred to them as I talked. When I had finished, I said, "I didn't want to tell you. These things are not always completely accurate, you know, and at such a time . . . My mother insisted, though. She said it was important. I hope you don't think I'm crazy, but she really does have a gift. I don't want to go into it right now, but I could tell you stories."

Sandra looked straight at me, and there was calm behind the trouble in her eyes.

"I don't think you're crazy," she said. "I don't think you're crazy at all. I'm glad you told me. If she sees anything else, please tell me."

I promised I would. I was returning to my car and Sandra called out, "Wait."

She came up to me and spoke in a low tone as if now she was the one who didn't want to be overheard.

"When you talk to your mother again, tell her I said thank you. And tell her I said hello. Tell her that I feel like I know her."

I drove home feeling relieved and more than a little puzzled. Sandra had seemed to know more about what I had told her than I did.

Time, as it turned out, would prove Mama right.

Chapter Fifteen

THE MEETING BETWEEN THE COMMUNITY and the police was delayed several times. It finally took place on a weekday evening a week and a half after Jon's death. We met in a conference room in The Other Barn, a community building that was once a real barn with a real hayloft and large brick silo and had been converted into village offices. Sandra didn't come.

Green laminate tables, pushed together, filled half the meeting room. Most of the two or three dozen attendees easily could have sat around the tables. Instead, only eight of us sat there. Police Chief Fred Chaney and the county's state's attorney, Bill Hymes, sat at one end next to three men I didn't recognize. Claudia Hollywood and I sat across from them, a dozen feet away. Ginny Thomas, our state delegate, sat to my right. A cluster of plain-clothed and uniformed officers sat behind Ginny, and a few more sat behind the chief. Another cluster of young people and a few adults sat behind Claudia and me. A few reporters and other adults I didn't recognize were scattered throughout the remaining card chairs. To an overhead camera the arrangement would have looked like a standoff.

Ginny thanked everyone for coming, expressed concern at the serious events occurring in the community, and assured the group that anyone who wanted to speak would be heard. She asked for

decorum. Then she deferred to Chief Chaney for any opening remarks. Sandra's absence hung like a dark cloud.

Chaney, tall and thin, had senatorially gray hair and wore wire-
rimmed glasses that gave him a scholarly look. He remained
seated and said expected things. He was concerned, and intent on
getting to the bottom of the case. The community had to remain
calm. Then he said he had no particular agenda and was open to
questions. Ginny looked at me and I took a few folded pages
from my inside coat pocket. I was nervous, so I read from the remarks I had already forwarded to Chief Chaney.

I said we were concerned that a premature ruling of suicide had
prejudiced the investigation of Jon's death. We were also concerned about stories that were surfacing about police harassment
and abuse of young people in the community. I asked that the ruling of suicide be changed until an independent investigation could
be completed. I added that Jon's family hadn't been treated very
well since his death. When I was finished you could have cut the
silence with a knife, so I moved on to specific questions.

The meeting fell into a pattern. I asked a question and Chaney
had an answer. It soon became apparent that no progress would
come of the meeting, and I found myself simply going through
the motions.

I asked Chaney what, in his professional opinion, was the sta-
tistical likelihood that an identical twin would commit suicide,
and he laughed.

"I'm not a psychologist," he said. "I'm a professional police
officer. I don't have anything to go on but facts."

I asked why the body was taken straight to a funeral home
without an autopsy. He answered that the county medical examiner had ruled that it was a suicide, and the police had no reason
to disagree. It was a school day, he said, and the police had
worked quickly to avoid upsetting the children, who would be arriving soon.

I asked why the scene had not been searched thoroughly and
the area had not been roped off. He said Detective Rudacille had

searched through the garbage cans and around the vicinity and had located nothing of significance. He said the area was clean and there had been no signs of a struggle and no indications of foul play.

I asked why Jon's death had not been treated similarly to a recent instance when a student had shot himself while on the phone with his girlfriend and had left a suicide note, and the police had roped off the area and had not made a ruling of suicide for several days. He said every case was different.

State's Attorney Bill Hymes introduced himself. He was about five-eight and looked like an aging bulldog. By then over a thousand people had signed the petition, and Hymes said, "I just wanted to inject that, in response to the petition I have received, and the considerable public interest generated by this case, my office has made the determination that Carl Jonathan Bowie's death is to be officially considered as 'unattended' rather than as a suicide."

Chief Chaney cleared his throat. "I want to point out," Chaney said, "that we have an honest difference of opinion here. Mr. Hymes sees the death as unattended. My department still believes it was a suicide and will continue to do so until such time as evidence is presented to the contrary."

"With all due respect," I said, "if the chief of police thinks it's a suicide, and the officers investigating the case are sitting here listening to you say it, then it doesn't seem very likely that we're going to get anywhere other than a conclusion that it's a suicide, whether it is or not."

Chaney's face reddened slightly. "We are quite capable, Mr. Parrish," Chaney said, spitting my name at me, "of conducting an objective investigation."

"But the investigator in charge of the case told a young man during a taped interview that he thinks Jon committed suicide. It seems to me that he's not leaving the door open for other possibilities."

A tall, thin man with stooped posture and a weary, concave face practically jumped from his seat behind Ginny. "I'm Detective Rudacille," he said, "and I want to ask you something. Don't you have an opinion about what happened to Jon Bowie?"

"No sir. I don't," I said. "I don't think there's enough information yet for anyone to have an opinion."

"There's nothing wrong with having an opinion," he said.

I could feel myself getting angry, and I measured my words. "There is if you're investigating what happened. Do you think there's anything wrong with asking the mother of a dead child if she wants to come to the station and look at the rope?"

Detective Rudacille stepped forward, closer to the table. "There was no rope. There was a cable."

"I'm aware of that," I said. "I was repeating what I was told you said. Did you also say that this was your investigation, and that you would decide if there was going to be an autopsy? That this wasn't a movie?"

"Ms. Keyser was excited and angry. I don't think I would have said that."

A young man I didn't know stood behind me and interrupted politely. "Excuse me. I have a question." No one responded, so he continued. "If I had been Jon Bowie's only known enemy, and if Jon had told people that I had been stalking him the week before he died, and if he was supposed to testify against me in a few days, would you interview me?"

Rudacille's face flashed red. He leaned forward and shook a finger across the table. In a startlingly loud voice he shouted, "Listen, young man . . ." He swallowed hard and paused for several seconds.

The sudden outburst left the room uncomfortably silent, and no one spoke or moved as the detective composed himself. Then, in a calmer but still quivering voice, he said, "I can assure you that no police officer had anything to do with Jon Bowie's death."

The young man also paused, and then asked calmly, "Based on what? Have you interviewed him? Do you know where he was that night? Who can back it up?"

Detective Rudacille didn't answer. Hymes and Chaney moved on to other points, and the young man sat down.

I wrote "Who is that?" on a scrap of paper and pushed it over to Claudia Hollywood. She wrote "Sean Stewart" beneath my question and pushed the paper back. I folded it and put it in my coat pocket.

We went through the remaining questions on my list. Chaney doubted there had ever been a lock on the cable. He didn't know where Jon had been between ten-thirty and six. He thought Jon could have climbed the backstop with an 18 percent blood-alcohol level.

There was a final question I had promised Sandra I would ask.

"Has Jon Bowie ever been charged by the Howard County Police Department with any drug-related offense, including possession of drug paraphernalia?"

Chaney turned to the officers behind him and they whispered for thirty seconds. Then he turned back around.

"I am not able to determine at this time that he has."

"Would you mind checking that out and providing Ms. Keyser with an answer? I keep seeing in the newspapers that Jon was charged with possession of drug paraphernalia. I don't know any place except the police department where they would have gotten that information."

Chaney turned and whispered again with the officers.

"No, he has not."

"Am I correct in assuming that means there have never been any charges against Jon Bowie that are in any way related to drugs?"

"That is correct."

I looked at Ginny and nodded that I was finished.

Bill Hymes stood and asked the three men to his left to stand. He introduced them as investigators from the Maryland State Police.

"The state police have assigned these men to my office to conduct an independent investigation. While I have complete confidence in our police department, I believe the citizens of this community have a right to an investigation with which they can feel comfortable."

Hymes introduced Captain Deane, a tall, gray-haired man, as

being in charge of the investigation. If I had known at the time that Deane was a longtime personal friend of Chief Chaney's, I would have been less impressed, but I didn't know. Captain Deane stood and introduced Sergeant R. L. Caple, a tall, black, athletically trim man. He had a firm, intelligent air that immediately impressed me as he addressed the group.

"I will be investigating and reporting to Captain Deane," Caple said. "When I have completed my investigation, I will report the results to Mr. Hymes."

The sergeant made a few more crisp remarks and sat down. I couldn't wait to tell Sandra how professional the state police investigators seemed.

I had prepared a closing statement and given it to Ginny beforehand. It lay on the table in front of me. Ginny looked at me and raised her eyebrows as if to ask if there was anything else. I looked down at the statement. It read:

> A young man in our community stands accused by rumor and innuendo of committing a serious crime. He and his family, and the family of Jon Bowie, deserve a complete and impartial investigation of the circumstances surrounding Jon's death.

I folded the statement without reading it aloud and put it in my inside coat pocket. I looked at Ginny and indicated with a slight negative nod that I had nothing to add. I was hopeful, but the police had not convinced me that they were willing to do their jobs.

The meeting ended and I was leaving when Bill Hymes approached me and asked if I knew any of the young people who had been at the Red Roof Inn. I said I did.

"The grand jury is supposed to hear this case in a few weeks," Hymes said. "If I had to present the case today, I'd have only one witness. Do you think you could persuade more young people to talk to me about it?" I said I would see what I could do.

Hymes thanked me in that distantly exuberant way politicians thank strangers, and walked away.

*   *   *

After the meeting, I was standing on the sidewalk in front of
The Other Barn, smoking a cigarette, when a man in street clothes
came up to me and introduced himself as a police officer.

"Mr. Parrish," he said. "There are some of us who understand
what you are trying to do. There's only so much that we can do
officially. We have pressures that you wouldn't know about, but
we do understand. We'll continue to do what we can. You have to
do the rest."

He offered his hand, and his grip was firm. We shared a long
and mutually unblinking moment of eye contact. I wasn't too
sure what he thought he understood that I was trying to do, but I
was comforted that he thought he did, and that he found it important to say it.

If anyone were to ask me the name of the police officer who
spoke to me that evening after the meeting, I would have to plead
what I've come to think of as the president's defense. It's what
several people who were President of the United States during
my generation have said when they found themselves in poten-
tially sticky situations.

I don't remember.

On the Sunday following the meeting, the county insert in the
Baltimore Sun carried a short, boxed correction. It said that the Associated Press had provided incorrect information about the charges
against Jon, and the correct charges in connection with the motel incident were disorderly conduct, resisting arrest, and obstruction.

There was no other clarification.

Chapter Sixteen

THERE WAS SOMETHING ABOUT SERGEANT CAPLE of the Maryland State Police that reminded me of a childhood friend of mine named Bucky.

After Bucky returned from Thailand where he had served in the Air Force during the Vietnam War, and I was finishing up at the University of North Carolina, Bucky told me that he wanted to be a police officer.

My family had moved to the outskirts of Durham, and Bucky and I sat on the front stoop overlooking the large front yard where we had played neighborhood football as kids. Bucky was recently married, and his wife Molly and his mom and dad and Molly's mom and dad were very much against his choice of careers. They had their natural concerns, Bucky explained. They were afraid he would get killed and, if not, everyone knew that being a police officer could put terrible strains on a marriage. Bucky could make more money with any number of other offers.

"I know in my heart that I'm a police officer," Bucky said. "I can feel it. It's who I am."

Bucky was about as naturally inclined to talk about his innermost feelings as he was to get naked at a funeral, so I knew he had already made up his mind. He was just building up the courage to tell Molly and both families.

Bucky became a police officer, and Jane and I got married and moved into a little cabin in the woods until we could finish school. Sometimes Jane and I went over to Bucky and Molly's apartment for dinner and board games, and sometimes they came to our place. We were sitting in their living room watching television on the night of the first moon landing.

One evening in a time when a popular term for a police officer was *pig*, I was sitting at Bucky's kitchen table and he told me how a woman walked past him on the sidewalk of the main street in Chapel Hill and spit on his badge and shouted, "Pig." He didn't know her and she didn't know him. He just walked on.

Chapel Hill is a college town, and you would expect a higher than normal education level, but Bucky said she had done it so I believed it. There was hurt and bewilderment in his eyes as he said, "Why would someone do that?" He wasn't asking for a response so much as he was trying to figure it out for himself.

I had been living in Maryland a year or two when a mutual friend called to tell me that Bucky was in trouble. It was in the local paper in Chapel Hill and even in the Durham and Raleigh papers and on television stations all around that Bucky had been charged with some sort of sexual harassment, which was a hot, new topic at the time. By then, Bucky had risen to the rank of captain and was being groomed to be the next chief of police.

I called and asked, "What happened?"

"I don't really know," he said.

A female officer had resigned to take a job in Durham. During her exit interview she was asked as a matter of form if she had any problems with the department. She said Bucky had offended her in some way.

I asked, "In what way?"

"They haven't told me. Maybe I told a joke she didn't like. She was in some of my training classes and you know me, I don't watch every word that comes out of my mouth. I've thought it over a thousand times, and I just can't come up with anything."

Over the next several weeks I spoke on the phone with Bucky

or Molly every few nights. A group of people marched through town with signs demanding that Bucky be fired. He got an attorney, and the attorney told him not to talk to the press.

I asked, "Is that smart?"

"It is for me. I'm not that good with words, and the press would just chew me up and spit me out. I intend to come out of this still being a police officer, and with my family intact. That's all. The rest is something I can't do anything about."

The chief of police eventually did ask Bucky to resign. I asked Bucky how it felt to have the man who was grooming him for his job ask him that. Bucky said the chief was only doing what he had to do. He felt sorry for his chief for being put in that position. I asked if he was considering resigning and, without hesitation, he said, "No, I couldn't do that."

The chief of police eventually told Bucky that if he wouldn't resign, then he would have to take a demotion to lieutenant.

I asked, "What did you say?"

Bucky's voice cracked at first, and then was firm again.

"I said I was the best captain in the department, and the chief knew it. I said that if I was busted to lieutenant, then I was going to be the best lieutenant in the department. I said they weren't going to run me out just because I'm suddenly some sort of embarrassment. I said that I'm a police officer. It's who I am. And if they want to take it away from me, then they'll have to fire me and find out then what I'll do about it."

Bucky didn't get fired, but he did get busted to lieutenant, and he stuck with the job. The department insisted for political reasons that he undergo psychiatric counseling. He resisted vehemently for a while. He eventually relented and said he was damned if it hadn't actually helped him some.

After a year or so the furor died down. It was not the kind of thing Bucky and Molly could forget, but they found out who their friends were, and they survived it.

I can't put a finger on exactly what it was about Sergeant Caple of the Maryland State Police that reminded me of Bucky.

Maybe it was his proud, soft-spoken, confident manner. Maybe it was something I thought I saw in his eyes, or heard in the tone of his voice. I don't know. All I know for sure is that I had so much hope.

Mama called. "Is there a tunnel near where Jon was found?"

"There are tunnels all over Columbia. Columbia has bike paths that go all over the place. There are hardly ever any bicycles on them, but people walk on them and they're called bike paths. They go through tunnels under the streets. There are probably a few near where Jon was found."

"Are they more square than round?"

"Yes. I think most of them are sort of square. Maybe all of them."

"I see a tunnel. There are what look like steps off to one side, and a rocky front. There's some kind of structure nearby that's like most of a rectangle, like a carport. I don't know if it's a carport, but that's the shape of it. If you're facing the tunnel, it's like the tunnel is up to the left and the carport, or whatever that is, is down in the right corner."

"I suppose I could find that. What does it mean?"

"I don't know. It's what I see. And there's another thing. Inside the tunnel, it's light and then dark."

"You mean like—"

"I don't know what it's like. It's light and then it's dark. And wheels turning. I don't know if it's near a road, or if it's the wheels of justice turning. There's also a mechanical thing that I see sometimes. It has a round part in the center and teeth around the round part."

"You mean like some sort of mechanical lift?"

"David," she said, as if to remind me that she was not mechanically inclined.

"Sorry."

I started saying good-bye, which anyone raised in the South knows takes more than a sentence to accomplish, and Mama interrupted me.

"Sandra didn't go back to work yet, did she?"

"No, ma'am," I said. "But she's thinking about it. She can't stay home forever."

There are dreams, and there are dreams. Some are pale and vague, and you wake in the morning trying to recall them, if you remember them at all. Others are vivid and startlingly clear. You sit straight up in the middle of the night, your heart pounding fiercely, knowing you'll never forget.

I was coming out of a building that I knew to be a courthouse. It was a large, redbrick building with white, fluted columns. Twenty or more wide steps led down to a spacious, brick-surfaced courtyard.

I came down the steps alongside Sergeant Caple of the state police. Several of Jon and Mickey's friends were also leaving in small groups. Something had been decided inside the courthouse, and the kids and I were not satisfied. Only Sergeant Caple seemed happy with the decision, as if he had done his job and the outcome was none of his concern.

The backstop stood off to one side in a large circle of dirt in a far corner of the courtyard. I didn't want to leave, so I climbed the backstop to rest and wait. I lay chest-down on top of the back-stop, arms stretched out. I was self-conscious about being on the backstop. It seemed somehow inappropriate, disrespectful, but I was there, looking down through the wire at the others.

Sergeant Caple walked past underneath, stopped, and looked up at me through the wire. He said matter-of-factly, "Jon will call you."

With unhesitating calm and certainty, I said, "I know."

I sat bolt upright, my heart pounding so fiercely I could hardly breathe. I shook my head violently back and forth, trying to forget, but I couldn't. I sank back into the pillow and stared through the darkness at the ceiling.

I half-expected the phone to ring.

Chapter Seventeen

As GOOD A PARENT COACH as I ever had the misfortune of coaching against was a fellow by the name of Charlie Brown. I'm not making that up. That was his real name. Charlie was a gruff, good-hearted sort with a thick shock of premature white hair and a gravelly voice that sounded like a loud whisper that only you and anyone within thirty yards would hear.

Charlie had two sons who were legitimate all-stars every year. His older son, Andy, was a real scrapper and a little on the small side. Andy eventually gave up organized ball and became a state wrestling champion for Wilde Lake High School. When he graduated, he went to college in Cleveland.

The night after Jon died, the kids at Sandra's had mentioned a Wilde Lake wrestler. A grand jury was expected to meet soon to consider whether to press charges against three of the police officers involved in the motel incident. Jo Glasco was preparing a list of witnesses to testify before the grand jury, and she asked if I could find out more about the encounter the wrestler and his friends had with the police. I agreed, thinking that Andy would know about it. I called Charlie to get Andy's number in Cleveland and, as luck would have it, Andy was home and answered the phone. I asked if he had heard the story.

"You could say that," Andy said. "I was one of them."

Charlie lived in a town house complex near the town mall. I

drove over one evening after work and Charlie was in the parking lot underneath a car. He dragged himself out and stood up, wiping grease off his hands. We shook and exchanged greetings, and he pointed to his front door and said, "Listen, if you're intent on pursuing the Bowie thing, watch your back."

"What do you mean?"

"I didn't know about the police around here," he said, "until this thing happened with Andy. I'm serious. Watch your back."

Andy answered the door and led me through the house into their small backyard where we sat on a green metal glider and talked. Eighteen months earlier, Andy and about two dozen other young people attended a party at a friend's home. Around 1:00 a.m. Andy left the party to drive three friends home. His friends had each drunk several beers at the party, but Andy didn't drink anything because it was his turn to be the designated driver.

Soon after leaving the party, Andy saw another very drunk friend sitting on a curb near a police car. Andy parked and, as they approached, another police car arrived. At this time there were three officers present. Andy told an officer sitting in a police car that they knew his friend on the curb.

"Can I take him home?" Andy asked, and the officer said he could.

They helped the friend to his feet and another officer walked up and asked, "What the hell are you doing?"

Andy looked at the first officer and said, "He said I could take him home."

"I didn't say you could take him anywhere," the officer said, and Andy helped his friend sit back down on the curb.

One of Andy's passengers began arguing, saying, "You said he could take him home." As he and the officers argued, the drunken friend got up and started staggering off. One of the officers threw him to the ground, handcuffed his hands behind his back, stood him up, and leaned him against the police car.

The drunken friend said, "Take these handcuffs off me, you fucking pig."

At that, the officer pushed him forward and, with a foot, swept his feet out from under him, throwing him facedown on the ground, cutting a long gash on one side of his head, and the officers looked at each other, surprised that he had hit the ground so hard.

"What the hell are you doing?" a friend shouted. "You said we could take him home and then you said we can't? Then you throw him down?"

"Oh, you want to be a tough guy?" an officer said, and threw the friend against the police car two or three times. One of the officers grabbed him from behind and another officer hit him in the face and ribs with his fists, a forearm, and an elbow. They finally got him stomach-down on the ground and handcuffed his hands behind his back.

Another of Andy's passengers was yelling, and one of the officers shouted, "Shut up." They argued and he resisted as the officer tried and then successfully handcuffed him.

"You're going to jail," the officer said.

An officer came over to Andy Brown and the third passenger as they sat with their drunken friend.

"Leave unless you want the same thing to happen to you," the officer said.

The friend ran and hid in bushes where he could watch, and Andy started walking away. Officer Riemer arrived in a police car, and his car skidded to a stop. He jumped out of the car and shouted, "Freeze."

Startled, Andy, who was five-six and weighed 129 pounds, stopped and raised his hands over his shoulders. Riemer tackled him from behind, knocking him to the ground. Then Riemer pressed a knee in his back, jerked his hands behind him, and handcuffed him.

A paddy wagon arrived along with eight or nine more police cars, and several passersby stopped their cars and got out to watch. Officer Riemer yanked Andy to his feet, and Andy fell several times as Riemer walked him to the paddy wagon. Riemer shoved Andy up into the paddy wagon, and Andy's face struck the paddy wagon door, cutting him above his eye.

An ambulance took the drunken friend to Howard County

General Hospital, where he lapsed into a coma twice during the night. Later, he told Andy that he didn't remember anything after he left the party.

At the police station, a half dozen officers were waiting in the parking lot and they gathered in a semicircle facing the rear door of the paddy wagon. Andy stooped to step down, and an officer grabbed his ankle and jerked him straight out, parallel to the ground, jamming his cuffed hands into his back.

As the officers led them to the police station, they repeatedly pushed them to the ground and dragged them, shouting, "Get up." Inside the station, two officers took the most argumentative friend down one hallway, and two other officers led Andy and the second friend down another hall, still pushing them down and telling them to get up. The two officers kicked them several times as they lay on the floor of the police station. Other officers walked by and watched, and they might have kicked them, too, Andy said, but it was hard to tell who was kicking when they were on the floor.

They were put in separate cells with their hands still handcuffed behind them. After a few minutes, an officer came with the more argumentative friend and locked him in a third cell. His eyes were puffed up and his face looked raw. A piece of skin dangled from his still-bleeding chin. He said the officers had taken him into a room where they removed the handcuffs and beat him up.

Toward morning, Charlie came. He said later that one of the officers was too drunk to understand anything that was said to him.

Andy was charged with disorderly conduct, hindering a police officer, disorderly intoxication, resisting arrest, and assault with intent to maim. Charlie called the FBI, and the FBI concluded that there was not enough evidence to press charges against the police. Charlie hired an attorney and the police offered to drop the charges, but Charlie wouldn't do it.

Eventually, Andy had his day in court. He tried to tell what had happened, but the state's attorney kept objecting, saying his testimony wasn't relevant. Officer Riemer testified that he tackled Andy because Andy had a stick in his hand, which wasn't true.

Another officer testified that he pushed the drunken friend aside so he wouldn't get injured while they dealt with the argumentative friend.

"That wasn't true, either," Andy told me. "They threw him down while he was handcuffed and so drunk he could hardly stand up, and they did it because he called one of them a 'fucking pig.' He shouldn't have said that, but that was no reason to throw him down while he was drunk and handcuffed."

Andy was given two years' probation, required to participate in an alcohol assessment program, visit a shock trauma unit, and complete one hundred hours of community service. The judge admonished him, saying, "You're a small guy, but you've got to learn to control your temper. You're a loose cannon waiting to unload. Learn to respect police officers. You can't take the law in your own hands, and you can't get in the way of police business."

When Andy and I had finished talking, I closed my notepad and we stood up from the glider.

"There are some bad police in Howard County," Andy said, "and I mean really bad. I don't know if that's how it is in other places, but that's how it is here, and I don't want anything to do with them."

In June, a newspaper article announced a public meeting to discuss whether the Howard County Police Department should be accredited by a national organization. Sandra thought someone should go to the meeting and say something about the investigation of Jon's death, and about young people who were harassed by police officers.

I disagreed. I thought the accreditation process, as it was called, was a good idea. You tried to set high standards and live up to them. I told Sandra I wouldn't do it. I didn't confess that part of my reluctance had to do with stage fright.

I changed my mind one morning while I was shaving. I was so nervous about speaking in front of a room full of people that I decided, if I didn't do it, I wouldn't be able to look at myself in the mirror. Charlie Brown went with me to provide moral support.

We sat in a sizable audience in a conference room in a county government building. Before the meeting, police officials of various ranks stood around the room in dress uniform, some with yellow braids on their shoulders. Chief Chaney was cordial to me even though he had to know the kinds of things I would say. Several members of the national commission, including some chiefs of police from various parts of the country, sat at a table in the front of the room. Reporters and camera operators were scattered throughout the audience.

People who wanted to address the audience signed a list in front of the room and then waited their turns. I signed the list and returned to my seat, remembering something I'd read about how you recognize stage fright. The mouth goes dry and the heart pounds almost uncontrollably. My mouth wasn't dry, so I figured I had at least an even chance of not fainting. A parade of local politicians, agency heads, ministers, and relatives of police officers went up front to the podium and described the many merits of the local department. A large, blond man took a turn, and I leaned over and told Charlie I was pretty sure he was the minister who had spoken at Jon's funeral. I said, "Maybe things will start to get interesting now."

The speaker had a long list of good things to say about the department, and Charlie finally leaned over and whispered for half the county to hear, "I don't know. He sounds pretty kiss ass to me."

Then it was my turn, and that's when my mouth went dry.

Wires for a large TV camera filled much of the aisle, and as I approached the podium, I worried that if I didn't stop shaking, I might trip over them. Then I was at the podium and I said, "Gentlemen," and it came out in about three different octaves. I grabbed the podium and held on tight. My legs were shaking, my hands were shaking, and my voice was shaking. If my feet had been screwed down, I might have lost a few body parts. The thought actually went through my mind to keep one hand on my notes and the other on the microphone so, if I fell to the floor, I could keep talking.

I said, as intelligibly as I could in a quivering voice, I didn't appreciate it when young people I knew and trusted told me they were being harassed by the police. I didn't appreciate it when they said they had been kicked and pushed around inside the police department with other officers looking on. I said I didn't think the Bowie investigation had been handled very well so far, and I gave a few examples. Finally, I said the national organization would discredit its own reputation if it found these things acceptable and accredited the county police department. If the police department straightened up its act, I'd be first in line to support them.

It was pretty quiet as I tried to work my way back to my seat without stumbling over the camera cables. I saw no reason to believe I'd made any friends.

Claudia Hollywood spoke and did a better job than I had. She said she was a nurse and that police officers regularly bragged in the emergency room about hitting people and pushing them around. Andy Brown's attorney spoke, saying he'd seen too many cases of young people who'd been beaten up by police officers, and he couldn't support the accreditation until some unsatisfactory practices were dealt with.

Subsequent articles in the papers said the police department had received overwhelming support from the community, and there had been a few complainers. The local cable station played a recording of the meeting every few hours for the next several days, but I couldn't bring myself to watch it.

If it wasn't so sad it would be funny.

On the night of my nervous-quiver dance, I was leaving the county office building as quickly and inconspicuously as I could. Chief Chaney was sitting on a bench near the exit, surrounded by a small group of officers.

"Mr. Parrish?" Chaney called out, motioning me to join him. I walked over and sat beside him on the bench. The tone of his voice suggested he was concerned about my welfare and wanted to explain something he didn't think I understood. "These young people," he said, "are not as innocent as you think. They have a group, you know, and they get together in each other's basements and wear togas and drink. You should look into it."

He told me the name of the group, and I wasn't sure I had heard him right. I asked him to repeat the name and, again, it sounded as if he said, "The Fidos."

I said I would look into it, and I left.

A day or two later I stopped by Jim and Sandra's. Sandra came outside on the sidewalk and I asked if Jon and Mickey had been members of some group.

"What group?" she asked, confused.

"I think it was called something like The Fidos. Chaney said they wear togas."

"Oh, for goodness' sake," Sandra said.

When Jon and Mickey were juniors in high school, a friend whose brother was in a college fraternity started a fraternity at their high school. The friend had a 4.0 grade point average and eventually graduated from West Point. They called themselves the Phi Epps. Underclassmen carried seniors' books in the halls and such. They had sweatshirts made with the fraternity letters on them and wore the sweatshirts to school.

I asked Sandra, "What about the togas?"

"That was the night of the initiation," she said. "They wrapped bedsheets around themselves and paraded up the street." She pointed to the end of the parking lot toward the evergreens. "Jim looked out the window and thought it was a Klan rally until he saw that half the kids were black. After the parade, they got together in Jeff Phipps's basement."

Fidos.

I'm not psychic like my mother. Still, I do wonder if I am sometimes guided. I had started keeping newspaper articles about the Bowie case and, after the accreditation hearing, there were several. I was searching through newspapers when a seemingly unrelated article caught my eye.

A young man named Brian Bumbrey had escaped from a drug treatment program and the police were looking for him. The article described him as a cat burglar and said the police thought he was responsible for a rash of burglaries that had occurred since his escape.

I saw no reason for the article to interest me enough to keep it. Still, wondering why I was doing it, I laid it on the growing stack of articles on a table in the basement storage room. As I walked away, still puzzled, I told myself I could take it off the stack later.

Chapter Eighteen

APPARENTLY, THE INTERNAL AFFAIRS DIVISION wanted to file a complaint on Chong's behalf against Officer Riemer for charging Chong with possession of drug paraphernalia. An officer from Internal Affairs started calling Chong, asking him to come in for an interview. Chong had already taken off several days from work at his family's combination convenience store and deli, and he didn't want to have anything more to do with the police department. He suspected that the department was filing the complaint just so they could find Officer Riemer innocent and clear the record.

Chong had already been interviewed by the same Internal Affairs officer after the motel incident, and he had met with the state's attorney and appeared in court. Everyone official, it seemed, still acted as if he had done something wrong and they had done him a favor. He told the officer from Internal Affairs he'd already said all he had to say and if the police department wanted to do anything about Officer Riemer, they already would have done it.

When Sandra learned that Chong wouldn't talk with the police, she asked me to try to persuade him. I went by his family's store a few times and he finally agreed.

Internal Affairs must have found Officer Riemer guilty because a hearing was conducted by a police trial board, which is an appellate process in which three police officers review Internal

Affairs decisions. Reverend Wright went with Chong to the hearing. There were several police officers in the room, and what Chong remembered most was that when he testified that he had been charged with a pipe that wasn't his, and about his conversations with Riemer, the officers in the room laughed at him.

"They laughed at me," Chong said. "This is America and they just laughed at me. You think I can forget that?"

A split rail fence enclosed a small play area in front of the daycare center. It was the children's nap time and Sandra leaned against the fence with her back to the parking lot. Anne knelt in front of her, planting flowers. To someone approaching from behind, it would have looked as if Sandra was standing at the fence alone.

Sandra had worried about coming back to work. The warning from my mother more than frightened her. It had shaken her to the core. Still, she couldn't stay home forever. Each morning Jim watched until she drove away. She took a different route each day, constantly looking around and in her rearview mirror. She parked near the door and stayed in the truck until a parent drove up or someone inside looked out and saw her.

The man came up through the pines on the knoll, stepping quickly across the asphalt parking lot at a brisk, confident pace, not looking to either side. He had come within six feet of Sandra when Anne jumped to her feet.

"What do you want?"

The man stopped abruptly, and Sandra turned and locked eyes with him. He was well over six feet tall, and his hair was a mixture of gray and strawberry blond. He wore khaki shirt and slacks and stood in a stiff, military posture. A three-foot length of orange nylon cord dangled in front of him between his hands.

He stared at Sandra a moment, jerked his eyes toward Anne, then executed a stiff about-face and marched briskly back across the asphalt. Sandra and Anne watched in stunned silence as he disappeared through the pines and down the knoll.

Anne broke the silence. "That man was going to kill you."

Sandra shook her head violently back and forth to regain her composure, then turned to her friend. "I know," she said. "You have to promise me that you won't tell anyone about this."

"You're crazy," Anne said. "You have to tell the police."

"No. They'll think I'm just being hysterical. Then they won't believe anything and we'll never know what happened to Jon. Swear it."

"Sandra," Anne objected.

"Swear it," Sandra said. "I mean it."

"Okay," Anne said. "I swear it."

A few days passed before Sandra told me about the man with the nylon cord. We still were sorting out the nature of our friendship, and as she explained later, she hadn't decided whether to trust me with the story. When she did tell me, I insisted that she tell the state police. She insisted that she couldn't.

I practically shouted at her, "Who are you going to trust if you can't trust the police? How can they do their jobs if you hold things back?"

"They won't listen," she said. "They'll think I'm hysterical and they won't take the investigation seriously."

Sandra was at home alone a few nights later, and at around eight o'clock she picked up the kitchen phone to call Captain Deane, Caple's boss. She was hoping to get an answering machine. Then she could tell herself she had tried. As fortune would have it, Deane was working late and he answered.

"I have something to tell you," Sandra said.

She told the captain how the man had come up behind her from the woods with the cord in his hands, how Anne had jumped up and confronted him, how he had pivoted and walked off, and why she hadn't told Deane or Caple before.

When she had finished, Deane asked, "Why are you telling me this? If this really happened, you should be talking to Chief Chaney. It's not our jurisdiction."

"I don't trust Chaney," Sandra said. "That's why we asked for an independent investigation. He won't do anything."

"Chaney's a fine person," Deane said. "He and I have been friends for years. You should talk to him."

Deane told Sandra a long story about a police officer in his hometown in West Virginia. "People made up stories about this officer," Deane said. "People said he was a bad officer. He was just a big old boy, just like Officer Riemer. You're on the wrong track with Riemer. He's just a big old boy himself. Howard County has one of the finest police departments in the country, and the community is treating Riemer bad."

When Sandra hung up, she stood with her hand on the receiver, scolding herself. "Why did I put myself through that? He didn't believe a word I said."

A few days went by before I stopped by Sandra's again, and I asked if she had told the state police about the man with the cord.

"Don't talk to me about the state police," she said. "You don't know anything."

When Sandra finally told me that it was Jeff Phipps who had walked past the backstop at almost two o'clock in the morning, and he hadn't seen Jon's body, I walked next door to Jeff's to talk with him about it. He wasn't home and I talked with his mother, Sylvia. She was a short woman of medium build with light brown hair. She confirmed the story and told me that Jeff was visiting a friend nearby. I drove to the address she gave me, and Jeff told me that he had seen nothing out of the ordinary as he walked past the backstop.

This conflicted with the claim by the county police and the state medical examiner that Jon died at around eleven o'clock. If in fact Jon died at eleven o'clock but he wasn't hanging from the backstop three hours later, then he must have died somewhere else. That would mean his death could not be a suicide. If he died later, after eleven, at the backstop, the police would have to give more credence to the banging and rattling sounds that John Sinelli heard.

Both Jeff and his mother told me that Jeff wanted to tell the county police about his late-night walk past the backstop, but the county police wouldn't talk with him. Then word went around that the state police would be investigating and the county police finally became interested in talking with Jeff, but he refused. He said he would wait to talk with the state police since maybe they were more interested in conducting a real investigation.

On several occasions when I stopped by Jim and Sandra's, one or two county police cars showed up in front of Jeff's house and officers got out and knocked on the door. I watched through Sandra's kitchen curtains, and the officers always eventually turned and walked away.

Then the state police got involved. Sandra told me Jeff talked with them about his walk past the backstop that night.

Two days after the state police began investigating, at nine-thirty at night, a Howard County detective picked up the young woman who had dropped Jeff off. Then the detective drove her to the school. The lights behind the school were off that night, but even with the lights out the detective concluded that there was no way Jeff could have walked behind the backstop without seeing someone hanging there.

With passing time, and after conversations with various investigators and attorneys, Sandra became aware that items were missing from Jon's belongings. There was the red key tag with the house key on it. Jon's belt was also missing. It was a reversible brown and black belt with a designer buckle. Sandra distinctly recalled that Jon had made a point of not fastening his belt too tightly before leaving home that final evening, and when he was found he was not wearing a belt.

"And his shoelaces were untied," Sandra told me. "Jon wouldn't even walk around the house with his shoelaces untied. It's the kind of thing a mother would notice."

Sergeant Caple stopped by Sandra's every few days, gathering information and updating her on the investigation. One day at her kitchen table, Caple explained to Sandra that he would present the results of the state police investigation to the county grand jury. He was a professional, he told her, and it would be better if she left the investigative testimony to him. Sandra gave this suggestion no particular thought, and she agreed.

I stopped by one afternoon and as she told me that she had discussed the missing items with Sergeant Caple, she added that a camera she had loaned Jon was missing, and the tape to his answering machine. I hadn't heard this before, and I asked, "Have you told Caple?"

"I only just remembered them myself," she said. "Besides, he can't be trusted. My friends told me."

I wanted to know, "What friends?" and she stared at me across the table and didn't answer.

On the Fourth of July, several dozen young people and a dozen or so adults attended an evening vigil at the backstop. Mickey and a couple of friends traveled from West Virginia where he was staying with his grandparents. People talked in small groups as TV reporters and camera operators waited near news vans in the parking lot for the ceremony to begin. Word had come second-hand from the police that they would stay away.

My mother had thought that everything would come out in June, when Mickey was supposed to be tried for charges related to the motel incident, but the trial had been postponed and June had come and gone. Now the trial was scheduled to begin the next day, July 5.

Sandra darted from group to group, thanking people for coming and fretting that the choir from her church had not yet arrived. The choir never came, and it was nearly dark when the crowd spread out around the baselines. A plump, young black woman from Sandra's church made a few consoling remarks and led the group in a prayer for justice and comfort. The news teams took video shots and left.

By the time the group began to disperse, a larger group was forming on the high school baseball field a hundred yards away to watch the annual fireworks display. People who didn't want to fight the traffic into town traditionally gathered at various good vantage points around town, and the baseball field was one such place. People spread out blankets, unfolded lawn chairs, and waited for the fireworks to begin exploding above the tree line.

A sizable group of young people gathered at Sandra's, coming and going to see the fireworks at various locations. Around eleven, the fireworks had long since ended and Sandra began to worry that Mickey had not come home. She returned to the field, and Mickey was talking with friends at the backstop.

"You kids get back to the house," Sandra scolded. "Are you crazy? You can't be hanging around here this late." In telling it later, Sandra said she had a premonition, an intensely strong feeling that the young people were not safe at the backstop.

"Mom," Mickey said, complaining.

"I'm serious," Sandra said. "You get away from this backstop. It's not safe here."

They grumbled, but Sandra insisted and they returned with her to the town house. Around one in the morning, Mickey had gone to bed and Sandra was serving sandwiches, chips, and deviled eggs to out-of-town friends who were staying over. There was a loud knock at the front door and Sandra answered it.

Lisa House, the young woman who had led the prayer at the vigil, was at the door. She was visibly upset.

"Somebody's got Mickey," Lisa said.

"What are you talking about?" Sandra asked. "He's asleep."

"He can't be," Lisa insisted, pointing toward the backstop. "I was just down there. Someone came up behind him and grabbed him. It was two men, a really tall man and another man. I saw it. You have to come with me."

"I'm not going anywhere," Sandra said. "Mickey is upstairs. Go see for yourself."

Lisa pushed past Sandra and went up the stairs. She came back down with a mystified look on her face.

"I saw it," she said.

Lisa was so upset that Sandra finally relented and started with her toward the backstop. Lisa's white Mercury Cougar was parked near the end of the street. They walked through the evergreens, and Lisa explained that she had been talking about religion with a woman who lived in the end unit. After visiting the neighbor, she had taken a stroll behind the school before going home. The field was dark and empty now, and Sandra and Lisa walked back through the evergreens.

"I saw it," Lisa kept saying. "I saw it."

As she got in her car to leave, she still looked puzzled and disturbed.

Jon Bowie was a born leader, a popular high school student, and an outstanding athlete. During his senior year, his varsity baseball coach selected him to serve as team captain— a position of honor, responsibility, and respect.
Photo by Sandra Keyser.

Sandra had this family portrait taken in Winchester, Virginia, when Mickey (*left*) and Jon were five. *Used by permission. © Lifetouch Photography.*

In the first grade in Wardensville, West Virginia, Jon (*left*) was a Dallas Cowboys fan and Mickey was a Washington Redskins fan. So teachers could tell them apart, Jon wore Dallas-blue sneakers and Mickey wore Washington-red. Just for fun, sometimes they switched shoes.

In the fourth grade in Wardensville, Mickey (*left*) often wore a Washington-red football jersey and Jon wore Dallas-blue. And yes, sometimes they switched jerseys.

on (*left*), Sandra, nd Mickey after moving rom West Virginia o Columbia, Maryland. *Used by permission.* *© Lifetouch Photography.*

Although Jon (*left*) and Mickey lived with Sandra, and their sister Carlen lived with their dad, the siblings were close. Jim Keyser took this photograph at a campsite in Ocean City, Maryland. *Photo by Jim Keyser.*

Mickey (*left*) and Jon were fifteen when they attended Carlen's high school graduation dressed stylishly as "cool dudes." *Photo by Sandra Keyser.*

As high school juniors, Mickey (*left*) and Jon joined a fraternity that another student started as a lark.

Jon as a high school junior during a home game at Oakland Mills High School. *Photo by Sandra Keyser.*

Jon (*left*) and Mickey were seventeen during their senior year in high school, and Carlen was twenty. *Photo by Connie Bowling.*

The decorated backstop on the morning after Jon's body was found. On close inspection of the roof, you can see the cut end of the cable where Jon's head lay as his fingers tightly gripped the wire. *Photo by Sandra Keyser.*

The tunnel where my mother said, "He ran and they chased him, and he came here to hide."

Inside Columbia's bike-path tunnels, the lighting typically creates a zebralike pattern on the walls where, as my mother had seen, "It's light and then it's dark."

Jeff Phipps said he woke up under this bridge, lying on his back with his feet dangling in the water.

Jon's commemorative paver lies in the walkway overlooking Columbia's Lake Kittamaqundi.

An old pamphlet left over from the 1990 primary election.
We handed them out by the thousands.

On the eve of the vigil commemorating the first anniversary of Jon's death, Chris Pons—the first baseman—and friends worked late into the night stuffing tissues through the backstop wire. *Photo by Sandra Keyser.*

County Councilman C. Vernon Gray and Carlen Bowie holding lighted candles at the first-anniversary vigil. *Photo by Jim Keyser.*

A small portion of the estimated
crowd of two hundred people
who circled the baseline
holding lighted candles
at the first-anniversary vigil.
Photo by Sandra Keyser.

In Memoriam: Rev. David Rogers
speaking at the first-anniversary vigil.
He had the courage and connections
to ensure that people in power
could not ignore this story.
Photo by Jim Keyser.

Mama and Sandra finally met at the celebration party the night before my son Mike's wedding. Growing up with a psychic mother was one of the greatest privileges of my life. *Photo by Jane Parrish.*

Mickey Bowie at home in Columbia, Maryland, in 1992, two years after
the death of his identical twin brother, Jon. *Photo by Sandra Keyser.*

Jane and me in 1992, attending a family wedding celebration in North Carolina.
Photo by Michael Parrish.

Sandra, Mickey, and
grandmother Ava Aylor
attending Mickey's
1994 graduation from the
University of Maryland.
Photo by Jim Keyser.

Mickey at forty years old
during a family outing.
Photo by Sandra Keyser.

Jim and Sandra Keyser, and their Himalayan cat, Priscilla, on the first Christmas in their new home after leaving Columbia. *Photo by Carlen Bowie.*

Home plate in front of Jon Bowie's headstone commemorates his love of and talent for baseball, and his prowess as a catcher. Someone has laid a penny on home plate, because Jon had a thing about pennies. The larger coins represent many pennies' worth of loss and fond memories. *Photo by Mickey Bowie.*

Chapter Nineteen

THE LARGE LOBBY of the Howard County district courthouse in Ellicott City leads to a long, wide anteroom where evenly spaced doors open into the courtrooms. At the end of the anteroom, an excited crowd of young people, including Mickey, surrounded a large, round-figured Latino woman with fiercely combed and largely uncooperative hair. Sandra spotted me and came over. She was clearly upset.

"Who's the woman?" I asked.

"That's Tina, Cristina Gutierrez, the attorney from Baltimore. I thought I told you about her. She's taking care of the criminal part of Mickey's case. Jo brought her in."

"What's all the fuss about?"

"Haven't you heard? Jeff Phipps was strangled last night at the backstop."

"What?"

"I called Sylvia and she says that he's at the hospital now. He'll try to get here in time to testify."

"So, he's all right?"

"I suppose. Tina says the county's playing games. The judge who was supposed to hear the case called in sick. They've brought in a man from Prince George's County who's supposed to be some sort of hanging judge."

I turned toward the circle of young people and tugged the attorney's sleeve to get her attention. "It seems that you could use a go-fer. What can I do?"

She sized me up, glanced at Sandra, and Sandra gave her an affirmative nod. "Court is in recess because of what happened to Jeff. When it reconvenes, I really need Jeff to take the stand. Go to the hospital. If Jeff can leave, bring him here. If he can't, come back and tell me."

At Howard County General Hospital, I approached a white uniformed woman in the reception area.

"I understand that you have a patient named Jeff Phipps?"

She gave me a guarded look and asked the nature of my interest. I explained that Jeff was scheduled to testify in a court case, and I had come to offer him a ride if he could be discharged.

"Wait here," she said, and she hurried away.

An authoritative black nurse came into the waiting room. "You were asking about Jeff Phipps?"

I explained again and she said, "Listen, that is a terrified young man. If I discussed it with you, I could lose my job. In fact, I'd rather not give you my name." As she said it, she raised one shoulder and extended her chest, conspicuously accentuating her name tag. She was Yvonne Last, the same woman who had spoken with Jon when he was seen for the injuries he suffered at the motel. "I will tell you this," she said, returning to normal posture. "The attorneys in this case should subpoena his medical records."

"I'll tell them. Where's Jeff?"

"Two friends of his picked him up a few minutes ago. It was my understanding they were taking him to the courthouse."

I thanked her and left. As I pulled into the courthouse parking lot, John Hollywood was driving out with a carload of young people. We stopped beside each other and rolled down our car windows.

"The trial is postponed," John said. "Everybody's meeting at Jo Glasco's office. Follow me."

I wasn't sure I was invited to the attorney's office, but I wanted to know what had happened. I made a U-turn and followed John to an office park in north Columbia. Mickey's friends and Sandra, John, Claudia, and attorney Jo Glasco and I crowded into Glasco's waiting room. Mickey hadn't come. He and the two friends from West Virginia had gone back to his home.

Glasco explained to Mickey's friends that they were involved in a serious matter and it was absolutely essential that they behave themselves and not get so much as a parking ticket. The county was, in her opinion, not taking the situation seriously and had indicated, in fact, that it would do anything it could to discredit those who had been at the motel. As she explained, Attorney Cristina Gutierrez arrived in a flurry. She brushed through the crowd and began making telephone calls at the most removed of two secretarial desks.

Jeff Phipps arrived in the company of two friends. One, Sean Stewart, was the young man who had stood up at the meeting with the police. All conversation stopped and Gutierrez hung up the phone.

Jeff's face was flushed and he held his chin close to his chest, as if he was shy about all the attention focused on him. The young people began excitedly questioning him about what had happened. The initial burst of questions died down and Jeff talked about it in a low, even voice.

He had stopped at the backstop the night before on his way home. He was nervous about testifying at Mickey's trial, and he had gone there to calm down and to—he hesitated and turned slightly away—say good night to Jon. He had no sooner sat down on the team bench along the third baseline when he felt a cord or rope around his neck, pulled so tightly he couldn't breathe. The cord was pulled up and back, and he had no choice but to stand. Someone marched him across the grass beside the school, across the street, and along a bike path through the woods. He tried several times to turn and see who was holding the cord, but each time he tried his assailant pulled the cord tighter.

His knees became limp and he thought he would faint. Something sharp kept poking his back, urging him forward. He thought he was going to die, and he wanted to leave a trace. He tried to stagger off the bike path, to leave a footprint, but he couldn't. After several minutes he did faint.

When he woke, he was alone, lying on his back in the dirt under a wooden bridge in the woods where a bike path crossed a creek. He crawled out from under the bridge and ran to a friend's house and woke the friend, who called the police and an ambulance. The police escorted Jeff to the hospital and he was examined. They released him and he went home, but in the morning he began hyperventilating and returned to the hospital. Friends drove him from the hospital to the courthouse, and here he was.

When Jeff had finished telling his story, he raised his chin and pointed at the marks on his neck. It looked as if something had been pulled tightly around the center of his neck in two loops. I tried to picture how quickly a person's hands would have to move to loop a cord twice around someone's neck.

Jeff pulled his shirt out of his pants and lifted it. The entire upper half of his back was covered with large welts and scratches that crossed each other in a fiddlestick pattern. They looked as if he had rolled, or been rolled, in grass with very large blades.

"They poked me in the back with something sharp," he said.

I said, "They?"

"I don't really know," he said. "The thing around my neck was so tight, and there was something poking me in my back. I thought there had to be at least two of them. I didn't see anybody."

He pulled down his socks and the area above each ankle was covered with more welts and scratches that looked like large grass cuts.

"What caused that?" I asked him.

"I don't know. I noticed it later."

His dress shirt had short sleeves and as he turned away from me, I saw a bruise the size of a thumbprint in the center of the muscle behind each upper arm. I took an arm and half turned it.

"What's this?"

He strained his head backward to look. "I don't know. I hadn't noticed that."

I turned him around and gripped his upper arms from the rear. When my fingers wrapped around his biceps, my thumbs rested naturally on the bruises.

"Were you grabbed like this?"

"No," he said. "Not while I was awake."

"Are you sure?"

"Yes. I'm sure."

The attorneys discussed taking Jeff to a professional photographer. Gutierrez phoned a friend of hers from Baltimore and asked him to represent Jeff.

"This is getting too complicated," Gutierrez explained. "Jeff needs his own attorney."

Before leaving, I told Jo Glasco what the nurse had said at the emergency room about subpoenaing Jeff's medical records, but in all the clamor I wasn't sure I had her full attention. She responded with a mechanical "Okay," so I wrote the nurse's name and her message on a slip of paper and laid it on her desk. I told her I had done it and departed. In hindsight I should have followed up, but I never did.

As I was leaving, Sandra said, "Come by the house." She looked tired and dazed, so I agreed.

When I got to Sandra's, Mickey's friends were letting themselves in and out of the front door, so I knocked and went in. Sandra was sitting at the kitchen table drinking a glass of water. I sat and loosened my tie, and she filled me in on what had happened in court while I was at the hospital looking for Jeff. Although she looked even more tired than she had at Jo Glasco's office, she was animated and excited as she spoke.

"Tina wanted to go ahead with the trial, but the county made a motion to postpone. Tina said that, under the circumstances, she would not object. Everyone was so upset."

"Did Jeff ever get there?"

"Yes. He was going to testify."

"What was he going to testify about? I thought he got into an argument with his girlfriend at the motel and left early."

"Didn't I tell you? He saw the officers arrive and hid behind a Dumpster at the motel. He saw everything."

"Where did you hear that?"

"Jeff told me, and Sylvia. I don't think anyone knew until a couple of weeks ago. Jo had him give a statement to the state's attorney."

"Why did he wait so long to let anyone know he was a witness?"

"Sylvia said he didn't want to testify, but then Jon died and he felt bad about not coming forward before."

"Did you notice anything about the way he talked today?"

Sandra looked pensive. "What do you mean?"

"It struck me as odd that he could speak with no particular difficulty after being strangled so hard that he fainted. Did that occur to you?"

"No."

"And those marks on his back looked like grass cuts."

"Like what?"

"You were a country girl. Remember how sometimes when you were a little kid, if you rolled around in the grass with bare skin you got large welts all over? They stung like hell the next time you took a bath. Of course, it would have taken some pretty large blades of grass to make those welts on Jeff's back. They were huge. I never saw grass cuts that big, but that's what they looked like. Lots of little scratches, big scratches, and red, swollen welts. Grass cuts."

"I don't know," Sandra said. "I don't guess I ever rolled around in the grass like that."

Two guys came running into the house and up the stairs, talking excitedly. I didn't catch what they were saying, but Sandra jumped from her chair and whispered, "Wait." She hurried out of the kitchen and up the stairs. After less than a minute she came back down.

"They've found something," she said. "I listened through Mickey's door and heard them telling him."

The two guys came running back down the stairs. One was Sean Stewart and the other was a pitcher I recognized from past baseball days.

"Whoa," I shouted, and they slowed and came into the kitchen. "What's going on?"

"I've been talking to Jeff," Sean said. "He told us where he woke up and we went there. We found some stuff that I guess the police didn't see."

"You didn't touch it, did you?" I asked, and he ducked his head.

"Shit. I didn't think."

"All right, where is it?"

He led us outside and removed a large, clear-plastic bag from the trunk of his sporty black car.

"How much did you have to touch it to get it in the bag?" I asked.

"Only at the edges," Sean said. He lifted a green, weathered snuff can from the bag by its edges. The bag also contained several cigarette butts and several frayed and faded pieces of orange nylon rope. The longest scrap was about eighteen inches long.

"There's lots of this rope around there," Sean said. "I just brought some of it."

Sandra was eyeing the snuff can. In an intensely controlled tone she said, "Jon carried a snuff can. We have to go there."

Sandra went back in the house to call Jo Glasco and came back out saying, "I asked her to call the state police."

Sean and his friend rode together and Sandra and I followed in my car. We turned into the neighborhood across the street from the high school and took a side street that ended in a cul-de-sac. We parked near the end of the street where an asphalt bike path led into the woods. A hundred feet into the woods, we rounded a bend and Sean pointed ahead to a bridge that crossed a small creek. "There."

"Wait," Sandra said. She pointed to a big patch of largebladed, waist-high wild grass beside the path. A circle of grass ten or fifteen feet across was flattened to the ground. "This grass looks like it has just been crushed," she said.

Mickey and his friends from West Virginia walked the quarter mile or so from his house and joined us. We searched the grass and the area around it, but we found only the usual array of forest trash: a broken bottle here, a shattered taillight lens there. Several pieces of the orange nylon rope were scattered about, some as long as three feet. The rope fragments were faded and frayed, indicating they had been laying in the woods for some time. I tried to imagine how Jeff might have rolled around and gotten the welts on his back.

After several more minutes of searching futilely, we went to inspect the bridge. "He woke up under there," Sean said, and we squatted and looked underneath. Sean crawled under the bridge and pointed to a place in the center where Jeff had said he woke up.

"He was lying on his back," he said. "His feet were dangling in the water when he woke up."

We followed the bike path back out of the woods. Sean recognized a neighbor wearing a jogging suit in a nearby yard. Sean mentioned the matted grass and the man said, "I walked through there last night at about eleven o'clock and the grass wasn't matted down then."

Sandra rode with me to Attorney Glasco's office. Glasco was waiting in the parking lot alongside Sergeant Caple of the state police and a county detective.

"This is their case," Caple was saying as we walked up. "We are investigating Jon Bowie's death. Anything recovered would be related to Jeff Phipps's case and would have to be turned over to Howard County."

This seemed like an overly hasty decision to me and I said, "I don't understand. If Jeff was strangled at the same backstop, wouldn't that suggest a connection?"

"It's their case," Caple said coldly.

"What if there were some evidence that related to Jon's case but not necessarily to Jeff's?"

"Like what?" Caple asked.

"Jon usually carried a snuff can, and there wasn't one on him when his body was found. The boys found a snuff can where Jeff woke up. It seems at least worth looking into."

"Mr. Bowie has been dead for two months," Caple said. "The snuff can could have come from anywhere."

"I know that," I said, "but you have to look at it to find out. The reason we asked for an independent investigation was . . ." Discomfort filled the air and threatened to bring the conversation to a halt, so I backed off. "The snuff can was closed," I said. "There could be a fingerprint on the inside cover. Then we'd know if it was Jon's."

Caple ignored me and asked Jo Glasco, "Where are the items?"

We got back in our cars and led them to the location. Sean and his friend were waiting, and Sean opened his trunk, took out the bag, and handed it to them.

"We can't take possession of these items," Caple said, and he handed the bag to the county detective. They spoke briefly with Jo Glasco and left.

Sean said, "You can kiss that evidence good-bye."

"What do you mean?" I asked.

"Get real," he said. "How old are you, anyway? The real reason Jeff went back to the hospital was that he got a threatening phone call. It upset him and he couldn't breathe. It was a man's voice. All the man said was, 'I see that you're still alive,' and then he hung up."

"Damn."

"It's not the first one," Sean said. "He was getting them before he was strangled."

"Like what?"

"One was, 'If you testify, you die,' and then the guy hung up. Another one was just, 'It's three o'clock.'"

"When was that?"

"A week or so ago."

"Did he tell that to the police?"

Sean shook his head with some disgust. "Shit," he said, dragging the word out into at least two syllables. "For all he knows, that's who's making the phone calls."

Chapter Twenty

THE DAY AFTER MICKEY'S JULY 5 court date was postponed, Jim and Sandra went to West Virginia to visit relatives and get away from New America for a while. Mickey and a friend went to a mountainous area in Western Maryland to help Mickey's uncle paint his house. Sandra lived with the desperate hope that at any moment an explanation for Jon's death might emerge, and before she left, she gave me her parents' phone number in case I learned anything.

That evening Jane and I were sitting at the kitchen table and I was telling her what Sean Stewart had said about Jeff getting threatening phone calls. Jane managed an office that provided resident services for one of Columbia's villages, and met regularly with a liaison officer from the county police. She told me about a call-tracing service the telephone company provided. You hung up after a call, picked up the receiver and got a dial tone, then pressed the star button and 69. This marked the last incoming call in the phone company's records. Each marked call cost a dollar and the police department could get information on the call. With some effort, a person's attorney might also be able to get the marked number.

"I should tell Sylvia Phipps about that," I said.

I called Sylvia but before I could explain she practically screamed, "Jeff has been at the police station for several hours and they took him to the hospital. They're trying to discredit him by saying that he's emotionally unstable. I need somebody to go to the hospital."

"Slow down," I said. "Why was Jeff at the police station?"

"They've been wanting to talk to him about walking by the backstop, but he told them that he would only talk with the state police. He didn't want to go, but they sent a detective who knows him. He took Jeff under his wing when Jeff got in trouble as a teenager. He talked Jeff into going."

"Why is he at the hospital?"

"They're saying he made up the story about getting strangled. Now they've got him in the hospital and they're trying to get him committed. He called me from the hospital and said I had to get him out of there. He said they took him in a room at the police station and kept him there for hours. They accused him of killing Jon. He panicked and started acting crazy just to get out of there. Can you go to the hospital and get him?"

"I'll try, but I'm not a family member. I don't know if they'll listen to me."

"Somebody has to go," she said.

"Is there a family member who can go with me?"

"I'll call Jeff's brother. He's a police officer in Baltimore."

"Fine. Tell him to meet me at your house. I'm leaving now."

Jane had gone upstairs, and I called up the steps to say I was leaving. A thought struck me, and I went back in the kitchen and phoned Barbara Stewart. I had met Barbara around Sandra's kitchen table and at the vigil. I had not yet made the connection that she was Sean Stewart's mother. Like many others, Barbara had offered to do anything she could to help, and she kept a list of phone numbers of local television and newspaper reporters who had covered the story.

Barbara answered the phone and I said, "I don't have time to explain, but Sylvia says the police have taken Jeff to the hospital. They're using some sort of special procedure to say he's emotionally unstable. Sylvia thinks they want to discredit him. Call

John Hollywood and see if he can come. Then call as many television stations as you can and meet me there."

All she said was, "Done."

I hung up and hurried out, grateful for people who know they
can ask later.

At five-foot-nine, Jeff's older brother David was no taller than
I am. He was younger, though, and in better physical condition.
We sat in my car in front of his mother's house and discussed
how to proceed. We decided that, since he was a family member
and a police officer, it would be best if he did the talking. I would
just be a witness and provide moral support.

I drove, and on the way I asked about the special procedure
that permitted an officer to commit someone.

"Basically," he said, "an officer can admit someone for a psychiatric examination if the officer thinks the person presents a
physical danger to himself or to someone else."

"So, if an officer abuses the procedure, it's his word against
the word of the person the officer wants to discredit."

He shot me a look.

John Hollywood and Barbara Stewart were waiting outside the
emergency room door. Barbara was slender with fair skin and
long, black hair that curled under at the base of her neck. Jon and
Mickey had spent a lot of time at Barbara's house over the years,
visiting her sons. She said several television stations were sending camera crews.

David identified himself to the receptionist and she immediately led him through the glass doors to the treatment area. I
wanted to call Cristina Gutierrez but didn't have her phone number. From a pay phone, I called the number Sandra had given me
for her parents in West Virginia. I told her the little I knew and
asked for Gutierrez's home number.

"You want her office number, too," Sandra said. "She works
late."

"This late on Friday night?"

Sandra insisted, and I took both numbers. Sure enough, Gutierrez was at her office. I explained as best I could what Sylvia had said about Jeff.

"You're at the hospital now?"

"Yes, and reporters from several television stations are on the way. Jeff's brother has gone in to see him. He's a police officer."

"I can't come," Gutierrez said, "so listen to me. If it looks like they are going to keep him, make as much noise as you can. Get him out of there."

"There are quite a few police officers here," I said. "I could get arrested."

I was pretty sure I heard her sigh over the phone. "The police can't tell you what you can say in a hospital," she said. "Jeff can't stay there. Do what you have to."

I hung up thinking that Gutierrez definitely had more nerve than I did. The door to the treatment area was open and an out-of-shape police officer about my age and shorter was standing just inside the door. I stepped inside, stopped, and looked around. I had no idea where Jeff would be.

"Step back," the officer barked at me.

"Excuse me?"

"Step back into the waiting room," he demanded.

"I'm looking for Jeff Phipps," I said. "His mother asked me to make sure he gets home."

"You can't come in here," the officer commanded. "Step back. Now."

We locked eyes for a long moment, and I stepped back out of the door. Despite what Gutierrez had said, he could use his badge to do anything he wanted and arrange an explanation later. I wasn't about to confront him.

A nurse came to the door, and I asked her if she could tell me anything about Jeff. I repeated the part about his mother just to add authenticity.

"I told you to step back," the officer barked.

"I did step back," I said. "I'm just trying to get some information for this kid's mother."

The nurse shouted, "Security! Somebody call security!"

I hadn't raised my voice, and her reaction startled me. Now I knew I could be thrown out. I took another step back and shouted, "Jeff Phipps is not spending the night in this hospital!"

I wasn't accustomed to confronting authority, and my legs started to tremble. I couldn't think of anything else to say, so I raised the volume a notch and shouted it again. The police officer took a threatening step toward me, and I turned and walked away. Gutierrez undoubtedly would have done it better, I thought, but at least it was a little noise. People in the waiting room were staring, so the hospital had to be aware of its liability in holding a patient against his will.

I went outside and joined Barbara and John. I told them what Sylvia had said and we compared notes on what we had heard about Jeff being strangled.

Jeff's brother finally came out. "They're releasing Jeff to me," he said. "A doctor examined him and said there's nothing wrong with him except that he's very frightened."

Barbara explained about the reporters, and David said, "We have to leave before they get here. I don't think it would be good for Jeff to face that. One of the officers is going to drive Jeff home, and Jeff will stay with me for a few days."

Surprised, I said, "One of the police officers is driving him? Do you think that's a good idea?"

"Jeff suggested it," David said.

"Your mom said he was terrified of them."

"Jeff says he knows one of the officers, and he wants that officer to take him home."

"Fine," I said. "I guess we'll be going."

David went back inside, and John, Barbara, and I walked to our cars together.

"This seems strange to me," I said. "First, Jeff's telling his mom to save him from the police, then he's asking to ride home with them. I hope we have this story straight."

"I feel bad about the reporters," Barbara said. "I don't like crying wolf."

We all agreed that we regretted that part of it.

Back home, I climbed into bed and Jane rolled over. "What happened?" she asked sleepily.

I lay back and clasped my hands behind my head.

"I'm not sure I know."

It was just a late-night thought, but if the police were so sure that Jon committed suicide, why would they accuse Jeff of killing him?

Chapter Twenty-one

ON ANY WORKDAY IN COLUMBIA, dozens of work crews mow, trim, plant flowers, and otherwise maintain the many paths, lakes, ponds, bridges, parks, pavilions, and grassy plots and fields known as "open space." "Open space workers," as they are called, would have tended the large grassy area that ran from the back of the high school, narrowed behind Jim and Sandra's, and widened into the side yard of another row of town houses.

When Sandra's brother Jack told me at the funeral that Sandra found strips of orange cord in her backyard soon after Jon died, I hadn't given it much thought. I assumed the cord had broken off of trimming equipment. When I expressed my doubts to Sandra, she explained that she had found two strips, three-foot lengths, just outside her backyard fence by the gate, and another three-foot length just inside the gate. She insisted they were too long to have broken off any equipment and, regardless, wouldn't have been left inside her fence. She and I visited local hardware stores and eventually confirmed that this particular cord was used in heavy-duty weed-cutting machinery. We bought a small roll, and she told me that it looked exactly like the orange cord carried by the man who had come up behind her at the daycare center.

One afternoon Sandra cut off a few feet of cord and went next door to see Jeff and Sylvia Phipps. Sylvia let her in, led her into the kitchen, and called Jeff into the room.

"Turn around," Sandra instructed Jeff. "I'm not going to hurt you, but I want you to tell me what this feels like. Close your eyes."

Sandra was shorter than Jeff, and she reached up from behind and looped the cord around his neck. She tugged lightly to tighten it, and Jeff jerked violently away and whirled around, wide-eyed, his face white as a sheet.

"That's it," he said. "That's exactly what it felt like."

In Maryland, circuit courts handle the more serious cases. On the third Thursday in July, a county grand jury began meeting in the Howard County Circuit Courthouse. State's Attorney Bill Hymes instructed the grand jury to consider two questions: Should the officers charged with beating Jon and Mickey at the motel be tried in court, and was there any evidence of foul play in Jon's death? In a hallway conversation with Hymes, Attorney Cristina Gutierrez objected vigorously that both issues should not be considered together, but Hymes disagreed.

A grand jury is a closed process by which a body of citizens decides whether to press charges against a person. The only people present in the large conference room where the hearing took place were the prosecutors, witnesses, and twenty-three jurors. Witnesses sat in a chair facing the jurors and prosecutors. They couldn't discuss their testimony outside the hearing room while the hearing was under way. They could leave the room to speak with their attorneys, but their attorneys were not allowed to enter the hearing room.

According to Gutierrez, a grand jury process is basically a charade that prosecutors use to get a public stamp of approval for decisions that they have already made. The prosecutor, who in this case was Hymes, decides which evidence the grand jury sees, which witnesses testify, and the order in which witnesses and evidence are presented. Later, the prosecutor can publicly wash his hands of a decision, saying that it was the grand jury's decision and not his. In the rare case of a grand jury that does not decide in the prosecutor's favor, it's called a runaway grand jury.

I took off work a few hours each day during the hearing and hung around the courthouse. I was optimistic that the grand jurors would learn even more than I had heard about the motel incident and would see that experience very much as I saw it. No one, I thought, wanted police officers hitting people unnecessarily or grinding people's faces into sidewalks with their boots. As for whether someone, police officer or not, should be held responsible for Jon's death, that, too, seemed like a no-brainer. Still, because the young people couldn't talk about what was taking place until it was over, I didn't learn much at the time about what happened in the hearing room. In truth, I didn't learn all that much later, because witnesses came and went and got on with their lives.

I did eventually hear a discouraging anecdote about a conversation that Hymes had that first day over lunch with two high-ranking police officers. The conversation took place at a small sandwich shop near the courthouse. As luck would have it, a person I know was having lunch there at the same time. Hymes laughed out loud and told the officers, "I'll guarantee you that no police officer will be indicted for anything in the Bowie case."

Some would argue that there was nothing unethical in Hymes's comment, that he could have been expressing his professional opinion based on his assessment of the evidence. Since the purpose of a grand jury is for private citizens to decide such things, and since Hymes would decide what the grand jury would hear over the next several days, I think the door is open for a different opinion.

Sandra testified on the first day, and she sensed hostility from several of the jurors. One juror asked why she kept staring at Office Riemer, and Sandra responded that she was not aware that she was staring at Riemer.

Hymes didn't ask, and Sandra didn't testify, about the matters Sergeant Caple had told Sandra to leave to him, such things as Sandra hearing shuffling sounds outside her house and someone shouting "Jeff" and then "Mickey," a car door slamming, the missing lock, someone breaking into her home the morning Jon's body was found, Jon's missing belt, the missing camera and answering machine tape. When Hymes had finished questioning her, he asked if there was anything she wanted to add and she said there was nothing. Sandra didn't want to interfere with Caple, and she assumed that Caple would testify about the things she had told him.

Mickey sensed similar hostility when he testified. Later, when he was legally allowed to discuss it, he said that jurors eyed him with suspicion. "It was like they already knew me, and they didn't like me," he said. "They just wanted to know if I smoked weed, if I drank, things like that."

Mickey left the hearing room convinced that nothing would come of the grand jury proceedings.

The grand jury met for two more days. On the evening of the third day, I joined Sandra and several young people at a table near the vending machines in the courthouse basement. Word had gone around that the grand jury had recessed for a week, and we were talking about whether we might as well go home. A large group of people led by a guard walked out a stairway door and past us.

"That's them," Sandra whispered with her mouth behind her hand. "That's the grand jury."

Several of the people filing past looked at us out of the corners of their eyes and walked hurriedly on with their heads ducked down. Some looked angry.

The grand jury expected to reconvene in a week. Jon and Mickey's friends had remained a tight group after high school, and before the hearings began word had spread among them that several of those who expected to testify were getting threatening phone calls.

One young man planned to become a state trooper. In planning for his career two years earlier, he had begun participating in ride-alongs with local police officers. One evening he rode along as Officer Riemer responded to a call from a woman who had reported a prowler. He and Riemer walked through neighborhood yards as the officer searched the area for the prowler. The woman caller was sitting on her porch some distance away, and Officer Riemer supposedly said, "I could shoot her from here and nobody could prove it or do anything about it." This observation disturbed the young man, and when Sandra heard the story she passed it on to Jo Glasco, who added his name to her list of witnesses.

Both the young man and his parents were out of town on separate trips when Glasco added his name. He returned home a day earlier than expected, and forty-five minutes later he got a phone call. When he answered there was a long pause and then the caller asked, "Is your father there?"

The young man said his father wasn't home and asked if he could take a message. The caller said, "Yeah, just tell him that Jesus called," and hung up.

Given such a strange answer, the young man thought maybe the caller planned to break into the house and had called to make sure no one was home. He didn't want to be in the house alone, so he called two friends and asked them to come over. By midnight they had discounted the call as a prank, and the two friends went home. The young man was still nervous, so he spent the night with his girlfriend and her parents.

The next day his parents returned and his mother called his girlfriend's house, looking for him. She asked him what had happened to the basement door. This was a surprise, so he went home to see for himself. A kitchen door that opened onto a staircase coming up from the basement had been kicked in from the basement side, driving the lock through the strike plate and splintering the molding in toward the kitchen. The young man and his friends had horsed around some the night before, so he called his friends and asked if maybe the three of them could have broken the door without realizing it. They agreed that it wasn't likely.

The next day, a Monday, the young man called the police. An officer came and inspected the door and took some fingerprints from a basement window. The officer said he had seen break-ins like that before.

"Someone wants you to know that they can get to you anytime they want," the officer said. "They want you to know you're vulnerable."

The police started calling two and three times a day over the next several days. One officer said he was with the Internal Affairs Division, and he wanted to know about the ride-along incident. The young man reported what he knew and said he was going to testify to the grand jury. The officer from Internal Affairs said he was calling from the courthouse.

Another witness who got an unusual call after his name was added to Glasco's list was a black seventeen-year-old high school student. I talked with him, and the story he told me was that, a year earlier, Riemer had stopped him at night as he was driving home from a friend's house. He was charged with driving with a learner's permit without an adult in the car, driving an unregistered vehicle, and driving a car with a broken side mirror. Each of the offenses cost him over $250, and his mother thought the officer had stopped him without probable cause and had piled up charges because he was a teenager.

When I discussed it with Sandra, I said it didn't sound particularly offensive to me. A kid driving on a permit should have an adult in the car, and cars should be registered and properly maintained. Sandra said the kid was holding back because he didn't know me, and what she had been told was that Riemer jumped on the hood of the kid's car and kicked out his windshield.

Attorney Glasco called the young man, and he agreed to testify to the grand jury. A few days later, while the grand jury was in recess, he got a phone call from a man who said, "If you know what's good for your black ass, you won't testify." Frightened, he decided not to testify.

The day before the grand jury reconvened, after an eight-day recess, the *Baltimore Sun* and *Washington Post* reported that the Howard County Police Department had become the 152nd police department in the nation to be certified by the Commission on Accreditation for Law Enforcement Agencies. The commission's report said the department had a good system, and mentioned the commission's awareness that the state police were investigating Jon's death.

The next day the grand jury resumed its hearings. A group of us sat on the rear seat in the large courtroom for an hour as the attorneys argued at the judge's bench. Tina Gutierrez argued that witnesses were being intimidated, and she wanted an open-court hearing to address charges that information was leaking out of the grand jury. She wanted to call Hymes as a witness. At one point an assistant state's attorney left the judge's bench and came back down the aisle, shaking his head. A group scribbling notes across the aisle appeared to be younger assistants in the state's attorney's office. The attorney looked at them and said something that made them laugh.

Alan Zendell, whose son I had coached on an all-star baseball team, was sitting next to the aisle, and I asked, "What did he say?"

"He said, 'I wish that Spic would shut up.'"

"I don't get it," I said.

"He means Tina."

The conference ended, and we went into the hall and waited for Tina. When she joined us, her face was dark with anger and she spoke with controlled intensity. "Denied," she said. "It's over. It was all a charade. They let me stand there and present a motion knowing all the time that the grand jury reached a decision this morning. They came in, voted, and went home."

We stood there a moment, taking it in, and someone asked for details.

Earlier that morning the grand jury had voted that there was insufficient evidence to rule that any officers had acted improperly in the motel incident. They would recess again and reconvene to reach a decision regarding Jon's death when the state police had completed their investigation.

Those of us who had come to support Mickey and his friends were stunned. We thought more testimony would be presented.

As we straggled out of the courtroom, a few stopped to speak with newspaper and TV reporters. It had been seven months since the motel incident, and three months since Jon died. I felt tired, dismayed, frustrated, but not discouraged. I still believed that, given the opportunity to hear objective information, most people would not condone unjustified police violence. I just didn't think the grand jury had heard it.

Chapter Twenty-two

JOHN HOLLYWOOD SET UP A MEMORIAL FUND. He bought T-shirts to sell with JON BOWIE written above the number 13, the number of Jon's baseball jersey.

Barbara Stewart contacted the local cable station, which routinely flashed poster-style advertisements and announcements for jobs, local events, business services, and such. When she hand-delivered the words, she requested a sign with white letters on blue and red bands so it would grab attention. The person who took the information said, "We've been wondering when you guys would get around to us."

The sign began flashing every few minutes on the local cable channel soon after the grand jury recessed, and it continued for several weeks.

PLEASE HELP US INVESTIGATE
THE DEATH OF
JON BOWIE

An editorial in the local paper suggested that the sign demonstrated a lack of confidence in the police department.

While the grand jury was in recess, waiting for the state police to finish its investigation, Sergeant Caple drove to Morgantown,

West Virginia, to meet with the medical examiner who performed the second autopsy. Jo Glasco accompanied him on the two-hundred-mile ride to ensure that the best interests of the Bowie family were protected. As a result of that meeting, the medical examiner wrote an addendum to his first report.

Sandra couldn't bring herself to read the autopsy reports, or the addendum, so she knew little of the details in them. I asked her to lend me her copies. I took them home, sat at my kitchen table, and read. I didn't understand a lot of the terminology, and that aside, reading them was a hard thing to do. I had to read them several times, setting them aside and then going back and trying again. I told myself I was just reading words, but I kept seeing flashbacks of Jon on a baseball field, laughing and throwing a baseball around.

The first autopsy, the one done in Maryland, found that Jon died of asphyxiation, which is not the same as strangulation. Asphyxiation is caused by a shortage of oxygen and results in death or unconsciousness. Strangulation is only one of the many things that can result in asphyxiation; it is an obstruction or compression of the throat, as with a jawbreaker, or a rope, and it tends to leave certain physical signs, which Jon did not have. Jon's skin bore no indication that he had strangled himself or been strangled; there was no bursting of the tiny capillaries in the eyes and no significant internal damage to the throat.

The cable left a bruise high on the neck under the chin, which the medical examiner determined matched the location of the cable on the neck. Slight abrasions and bruises, particularly on the chest and abdomen, seemed likely to have come from the wire on the backstop. There were no signs of struggle. Because of the examination, and what the report referred to as "investigative details," the death was ruled a suicide. What the first autopsy suggests is that Jon put the cable around his neck, gripped the roof of the backstop with both hands, quietly fell asleep, and suffocated.

Detective Rudacille no doubt provided many of the investigative details that the medical examiner said helped him make a ruling of suicide. However, it is important to note that Rudacille arrived at the scene after Jon's body had been lowered to the ground, so he did not see the body on the backstop. When Sandra took Rudacille to task for calling Jon's death a suicide from the outset, he defended himself by saying his opinion was based on the decision at the scene by the county medical examiner. However, the county medical examiner did not see the body on the backstop, either. He, too, had arrived at the scene after the body was lowered.

The second autopsy was done in West Virginia after the embalming, which the performing doctor did not see as a significant hinderance. He didn't have the cable, he knew little about how the body had been found, and he didn't have a police officer standing nearby to provide investigative details. He conducted a physical examination, but he did not do any chemical testing or other laboratory analysis.

The second doctor agreed that death was due to asphyxiation that, in all likelihood, was caused by the cable. The cable caused only one furrow. This made it highly unlikely that Jon could have been hanged at another location and moved to the backstop and been hanged again; this would have required that marks on the neck caused from two separate hangings overlap exactly, and that was virtually impossible.

It also would have been extremely difficult, the second report concludes, for one or more persons to stand behind Jon on the backstop, hold the cable, and then leave him there. Jon could have been taken unconscious to the backstop, raised onto the backstop, and the cable put around his neck, the report says, but nothing about the physical examination indicated that he had been unconscious. The doctor saw no signs of a struggle. It would have to be demonstrated that Jon was unconscious for such a conclusion to be reached, and without the results of toxicological tests, nothing further could be said about that possibility. It wasn't likely that Jon simply became entangled in the cable and fell; there would have been greater damage to the neck.

The second autopsy noted two bruises that were not mentioned in the first. A faint two-and-three-quarter-inch bruise rose vertically from underneath the right armpit and up the front toward the right shoulder. What the autopsy report didn't mention, because the examiner didn't have this information, was that this bruise, which looked like a mark caused by a thin rope or cord, could not have been caused by the rope used to lower Jon's body from the backstop. That rope was very thick, and police photos show clearly that the rope was tied behind Jon's back. If it had ridden up underneath the armpit, it would have left a mark on the back of the armpit, not the front.

The second bruise that was not mentioned in the first autopsy was low on the right side of the lower neck, too low to have been caused by the cable. It was four and a half inches long and shaped like a horizontal Y that opened toward the front-middle of the neck. The trunk and both branches of the Y-shaped bruise were each about a half inch wide. The upper trunk of the Y, and the point where the two forks met, were red, suggesting to the examiner that they were caused before death; the lower fork was yellowish, suggesting that it became visible after death.

The bottom line of the second autopsy was that the doctor didn't have enough information to form a scientific opinion about how Jon had come to be asphyxiated, perhaps by a cable, or how he had come to be on the backstop. He couldn't say it was suicide and couldn't say it wasn't.

In the addendum to the second autopsy, which the doctor wrote after talking with Jo Glasco and Sergeant Caple, the doctor said he was now convinced that Jon could not have slipped and fallen and somehow become tangled in the cable. Either he put the cable around his neck himself, voluntarily or involuntarily, or someone else put it around his neck. If someone else did it, then it would have been difficult for one person to have done it alone; two or more people would have had to do it. Jon would have had to be subdued in some way so he could not resist, or be unconscious or nearly unconscious. Although Jon's blood alcohol level was quite high, it was not high enough to convince the doctor that Jon could not have climbed the backstop. It could not be scientifically answered, the addendum says, whether Jon put the cable around his

own neck and then, being inebriated, unexpectedly lost con-
sciousness and slumped with the full weight of his body putting
pressure on his neck. It could not be answered, either, if he had
succumbed to some sort of suicidal impulse while intoxicated.
The final statement in the one-and-a-quarter-page addendum,
above the doctor's signature, read, "I cannot exclude that this
might possibly be a homicide."

I laid the West Virginia addendum on the kitchen table along
with the two autopsies. Why hadn't the Maryland autopsy mentioned the bruise at the base of Jon's throat, or the vertical bruise
at the front of his armpit? I didn't understand the bruise on the
throat, but I would learn eventually that it could have been
caused by a martial arts maneuver. If you rest your thumb on a
person's collarbone, at the base of the neck, and your forefinger
similarly on the other collarbone, and squeeze, you can render the
person unconscious without leaving a trace. If you squeeze too
hard, you might leave a bruise.

Even without that information, I could easily imagine at least
one scenario that neither autopsy ruled out. The Maryland medical examiner tested Jon only for recreational drugs. That left
open the possibility that someone could have drugged Jon, ren-
dering him unconscious. The neighbor, John Sinelli, had heard
banging and rattling from the direction of the backstop, my
mother had seen something like a mechanical lift, and Jon had an
unexplained vertical bruise on the front of his armpit. All of these
would be explained if someone had looped a rope around Jon's
chest, tying it in the front, not in the back as the rescue workers
had done, and used a common portable mechanical winch called
a come-along to raise his unconscious body onto the backstop,
and then put the cable around his neck. If I could imagine such a
scenario, certainly the investigators could—assuming, of course,
that they wanted to see it.

Chapter Twenty-three

BEING SO CLOSE TO THE NATION'S CAPITAL, it was not unusual that Sandra would have a friend who knew a homicide expert with the CIA. This expert read the two autopsies and sent word back to Sandra that something about the blood alcohol tests was out of order. There were four blood alcohol tests, which was standard procedure. A sample taken from the heart at the scene was labeled County. During the autopsy another specimen was taken from the heart and labeled State. Specimens were also taken of the fluid of the eye and from the urine. The results were: state heart: .25; county heart: .18; eye: .27; urine: .37.

I called my friend Bucky in North Carolina and asked what he could tell me. He asked a forensics expert and called me back a few days later. If I had my information right, he said, then one of the results was out of order, but that didn't necessarily mean anything. Tests could vary for all kinds of reasons. I gave him a few details about Jon's death, and he suggested that I was going off the deep end. "Young people have more violent, unpredictable reactions to alcohol than adults," he said. "A kid who would never consider suicide might have a few drinks, get depressed, and do it on an impulse."

I told him a bit about the motel incident and he said, "You've told me more than you might have meant to. You told me he was a good athlete. Athletes can be pretty cocky. They might bring something on themselves and not even understand what they've done. A police officer has to take charge of a situation. He doesn't always have time to explain every little thing."

I was angry at Bucky for a few days because he had not said anything that I wanted to hear.

One evening while the grand jury was still in recess, anticipating the results of the state police investigation, I was lying in bed waiting to fall asleep and I found myself wondering what it felt like to be Sandra. For a startling instant, I felt a rush of anger and fear and hope and despair and terror. It seemed to come from outside of myself, as if I had actually felt what Sandra felt. I had to drop the bundle of feelings from my mind the way I would immediately drop a package I had no idea was so heavy.

From time to time I became concerned for my own safety. Nothing specific had happened to cause my concern, but my mother had told me to be careful, Charlie Brown had told me to watch my back, and I could think of no logical explanations for the bizarre events surrounding Jon's death. I didn't tell Jane because I didn't want to worry her, but some mornings before starting the car to go to work I looked underneath for anything that might have been placed there and raised the hood sometimes to look in the engine compartment. Then I put the key in the ignition, closed my eyes, grimaced, and turned the key.

On one such morning, after surviving the engine ignition, I drove to work wondering what I had gotten myself into. I didn't like being seen as coming out against the police. I hated even considering the possibility that a police officer might actually have had something to do with Jon's death. I didn't like it, either, when young people I trusted told me they had been abused by police officers. I didn't like it that the county seemed to be turning itself upside down while I still had no idea what had happened to Jon. About halfway to the office I consciously chose to follow this path wherever it led, trying to stay as objective as I could without getting swept up in some overly emotional reaction, but without backing off, either, just because some people didn't even like it to be discussed. The exact words that I said out loud to myself were, "In for a penny, in for a pound." To bolster my resolution, I struck the steering wheel with my palm as I repeated it several times, convincing myself that I meant to stick with it.

Call it a weird coincidence, but pennies started showing up. I'd find them in the car, on the floor at the office, on the sidewalk. You name it. I once knew a man who had a responsible management position with a large telecommunications company. He would never pass up a penny. It was something of a joke with his coworkers, and we'd sometimes leave a penny where he could find it just to watch his reaction. He was a responsible, intelligent person, and I had considered this penny business an odd quirk in his personality that did no particular harm. Still, I wasn't thrilled that something like this seemed to be happening to me. At first, I wrote it off as coincidence, but there were so many coincidences that I couldn't help but notice.

For a long time I didn't mention this to anyone, not even to Jane, whom I'd usually tell anything. When I finally did mention the pennies to her, she surprised me and said they probably were some sort of message, a reassurance that I had assistance in what I was trying to accomplish. I also eventually mentioned the pennies to Sandra, who said the same thing had been happening to her. She hadn't wanted to mention it for the same reasons I hadn't wanted to. She said Jon had always had a thing about pennies. He would sit in his bedroom when he wanted to think and toss them against the baseboard. He had a jar filled with pennies.

In the morning of the Saturday that fell a week after the grand jury recessed, Sandra answered a knock at her front door. Lisa House, the young woman who said she had seen Mickey abducted at the backstop, was standing there, and she was visibly upset. Sandra invited her in and led her into the kitchen.

In a hysterical barrage of details, Lisa said that earlier that morning she was driving to a nearby interfaith center—a Columbiaconcept building where congregations of various churches and synagogues meet in different sanctuaries—to run an errand for her church. A police car began following her so closely she couldn't see its headlights in her rearview mirror. When she arrived at the interfaith center, she parked as close as she could to the building and the police car parked farther away in the same parking lot. She went inside and completed the work for her church, which took about twenty minutes. When she came back out into the parking lot, the police car was still parked there and a large man about six and a half feet tall was leaning against her car. He wore a plaid shirt, blue jeans, a baseball cap pulled low over his face, and sunglasses. Sandra, of course, thought of Riemer. Lisa said she was sure that's who it was. As she approached the car, the man stood up straight and spoke to her.

"Did you know Jon Bowie?"

"I might," Lisa said. "Do you want to sign my petition?"

The petition signing had ended by then, but he was looking at some leftover petition forms on her backseat, so that's what she said.

The man shouted, "Fuck that," returned to the police car, and drove away.

Lisa had participated in the backstop vigil and in a sparse sign-carrying demonstration in front of a county office building, and her picture had appeared on television news. She thought that maybe he saw her as some sort of organizer. When Lisa finished telling her story, Jim offered to follow her home. Sandra rode with Lisa and Jim followed in his van.

They returned home and had been there about fifteen minutes when the phone rang. It was Lisa. She said that soon after she got home she got a phone call from a man who didn't identify himself. The voice was that of the man in the parking lot, and he said, "I asked you, 'Did you know Jon Bowie?'"

"Yes, I did. Why do you want to know?"

"If you don't back off, I'll do the same thing to you that I did to Jon Bowie." Then he hung up.

A half hour later Lisa called Sandra again. "We have to end our friendship," she said, "and I can't have any more contact with you, but my family and I will pray for you."

On Sunday, Lisa approached Sandra in church and said her father had forced her to make the second call. "He has great fear for me and for the rest of the family."

Sandra said she understood.

A few days later, Lisa called Sandra at work and said she had decided to go against her father's wishes. She wanted to give Jo Glasco a statement about the incident and the phone call.

That was the last contact Sandra would have with Lisa for more than a month. Sandra tried several times to telephone her at her condominium or at her father's home. Sometimes her father answered the phone and said no one named Lisa lived there. Sometimes Sandra called Lisa's sister, and sometimes her sister said she would try to intervene with her father. Sometimes she told Sandra no one named Lisa lived there, and hung up.

Chapter Twenty-four

ON A WEDNESDAY TOWARD THE END of August, the grand jury met briefly, voted, and adjourned. Then Bill Hymes held a press conference in a county office building.

Mickey had recently returned from West Virginia in anticipation of the upcoming fall semester at a local community college. As Sandra was leaving for the press conference, Mickey told her that he wasn't coming.

"You know what they've decided. I'm not wasting my time."

A large audience of friends and family members, reporters, television crews, attorneys, and police officers waited while Hymes, an assistant state's attorney, and Sergeant Caple seated themselves at a folding table on a raised platform. Hymes leaned into a wide bank of microphones and read a brief report from the grand jury. The report concluded:

> There is presently no physical evidence or any other evidence that Carl Jonathan Bowie met his death through the intervention of any other individual.

Then Sergeant Caple read a brief report summarizing the state police investigation. Its conclusions were that Jon climbed the backstop himself, that he put the cable around his own neck, and that his death was determined, not accidental. However, there was no note and there were no witnesses, and it could not be determined what was on Jon's mind at the time. Caple concluded:

> Considering the absence of these factors, our findings reveal no evidence of foul play and the manner of death was undetermined.

Reporters scratched their heads and looked at each other. They asked a few questions and scribbled notes. Photographers and video camera operators walked around the speakers trying to get good shots.

That night a newspaper reporter called me at home and said he had found the decision carefully worded and confusing. He asked what I thought, and I said, "It sounded negotiated to me."

When Sandra had learned that the investigation was coming to an end, she was furious. Caple had promised to meet with her before presenting any conclusions publicly. Sandra called Jo Glasco and reminded her of the promise, and Glasco persuaded the state police to meet with the family.

The meeting took place two weeks after the grand jury ended. Only Sandra and Jo Glasco and their invited guests were allowed to attend. Once again, Mickey chose to stay away. He had told Sandra that he knew nothing would come of it.

We sat around a large conference table in a government building in Ellicott City, and Sergeant Caple and another state trooper handed out a seventeen-page report. We thumbed along as Caple read the entire seventeen pages aloud. The details get a little tedious, but these were the major points:

- The state police had found no fingerprints, including Jon's, on the vinyl cable.
- Two sets of fingerprints in Jon's car had not been identified.
- The state police had not learned where Jon was from the time he left his friend's house until he was found at the backstop.

- Jon had not drunk enough beer at his friend's house to account for his high blood alcohol level.
- Red wool fibers had been found on virtually all articles of Jon's clothing, including his underwear, and the origin of the fibers was not determined. Caple noted that such fibers were common.
- One blue wool fiber was also found, and no source was identified.
- Rust stains on the bottoms of Jon's boots and on his clothing probably came from the backstop wire, which was rusted.
- Laboratory analysis could not identify the source of grease-like stains on the calf area of the rear of both of Jon's pant legs.
- There was a small smudge of white paint of unknown origin on Jon's shirt.
- A .22 caliber bullet that was found at the backstop was not judged as being of an evidentiary nature.

Caple passed around several enlarged photographs of Jon on the backstop. It was the first time most of us had seen them, and Sandra said, "I can't look." We silently agreed with glances and nods to hand the photographs past her. Chris, the first baseman, slipped a few photographs inside his windbreaker. Tears began streaming down Carlen's cheeks, and she got up and left the room.

I followed Carlen outside to smoke a cigarette and to see if she was all right, and she wasn't. Several reporters noticed her standing alone and came over to ask who she was. I said only that the meeting was hard and they should leave her alone. I finished my cigarette and went back in the room. By then the passing of photographs was over.

Caple had interviewed Riemer, who said that on the evening before Jon's body was found, he had dinner with his parents and left at six thirty and went home. At eleven-thirty, he called a local bar and talked to a young woman who worked there. He went to her apartment after she got off work and they watched videos.

Her roommate showed up around three a.m. and, around four, Riemer went home. On the way he passed an officer who had pulled over a vehicle, and he stopped to see if the officer needed assistance. There was no mention in the state police report that Riemer was supposedly off duty the night Jon died or that several people claimed to have seen him in uniform that evening in Clyde's restaurant.

Ricky Johnson, Caple said, watched TV at home that night and couldn't remember if anyone called him or stopped by during the evening.

Caple turned a page and began reading a summary of several interviews with unidentified people. He said Jon had started drinking at fifteen, that between the ages of fifteen and seventeen Jon was usually intoxicated, and that Jon drank between twelve and eighteen cans of beer each day on the weekends and between three to six beers each weekday. I looked at Sandra, and her face had reddened and her eyes were fiercely intent. She said across the conference table, "That's simply not true. Who told you these things?" Sandra and Caple argued heatedly, and Caple never revealed his sources.

Caple said Jon was aggressive in high school and had suffered a broken hand and finger and a black eye as the result of various altercations.

"It's not true," Sandra said. "He broke his hand scuffling with his brother, and he broke his finger playing baseball. I've explained all of this to you. Why are you doing this?"

Caple ignored Sandra and continued. "He was known to have provided the names of drug users to a known drug peddler."

To say that Sandra broke into a one-sided shouting fit would be to understate the fusillade that followed. Caple sat expressionless as Sandra tore into him. She took a breath and I asked, "Where did you get this information?"

Caple explained how someone named Brian Bumbrey had violated parole and fled to California. The police arrested Bumbrey and planned to extradite him to Maryland, but Bumbrey told them that he couldn't go back to Maryland because two police officers there were selling drugs and had killed his friend Jon Bowie and would kill him, too, if he was extradited. That, Bumbrey said, was why he fled.

At the time, I didn't recall the article I had cut out of the newspaper two months earlier about a cat burglar named Brian Bumbrey, and I was dumbfounded. I leaned over and whispered to Sandra, "Have you ever heard of this Bumbrey person?"

No, she mouthed.

So far as I remembered, neither had I.

The other investigator said that Bumbrey had been returned to Maryland and interviewed. It appeared to the police that he was simply making up the story, but it had to be further investigated. "It is a serious matter," he said, "when two police officers are alleged to be involved in illegal drug activity. We have to take it seriously."

"Why is it in the report?" I asked, "if it's still not verified? Why are we meeting? Why has the grand jury already reached a decision? Is this investigation over or not?"

"It's what we know to date," Caple said. "It's a part of the information that was gathered during my investigation."

"But that's not what the report says." I put a finger on the sentence in my copy of the report and read it back to him. "It says '. . . known to have provided the names of drug users to a known drug peddler.' "

"That's what was said," Caple said.

"Let me get this straight. You believe this guy Bumbrey when he says Jon gave him names of drug users, but you don't believe him when he says the police had something to do with drugs, and with Jon's death. It sounds like you're being pretty selective about what you choose to believe."

"We're still looking into that," the other trooper said.

The conversation didn't seem to be going anywhere, so I changed the subject.

"What about the lock?"

Caple gave me a blank look. Alan Zendell explained, "Dave's thinking on that is that, if the cable was locked down and the lock wasn't found, Jon had to climb the backstop twice. He had to climb it once to go up and get the lock. Then he had to come back down and dispose of the lock in a way that it couldn't be found. Then he had to climb the backstop a second time to put the cable around his neck. If that's not the kind of thing an inebriated person intent on suicide is likely to do, and I don't think it is, then you have to consider the possibility that someone else was involved, and that whoever it was got sloppy and disposed of the lock, not realizing that the missing lock would discredit the theory that Jon killed himself."

"I spoke with the baseball coach," Caple said. "He said he didn't have any reason to believe the cable was locked down."

Sandra said, "He plays and practices on the varsity field. He doesn't have any responsibility for the field where Jon was found, which is the field where they play girls softball and little league baseball. Did you talk to the athletic director? She's the one who told the police that the cable was locked down. That field is her responsibility. She said she had checked the cable the week before and it was locked down."

"I contacted her," Caple said, "and she was too upset to discuss it."

So, that was it. The state police had asked someone who spent little time at the field if the cable was locked down, and the person who had originally said it was locked down no longer felt like talking about it, four months after Jon's death. End of subject.

The meeting by this time had gone on for a couple of hours, and I was feeling worn down. Caple completed his remarks about Jon's character with, "Known to utilize false identification to gain access to bars and purchase alcoholic beverages." I thought, *Who cares?* and didn't join in the argument that followed. I knew a woman who had manufactured fake IDs at the University of Maryland in the sixties and who eventually became president of a local PTA. It was becoming increasingly apparent that the state police investigation had been conducted at a third-grade level with no genuine motivation for finding out what had really taken place.

"I knew this kid a long time," I said, "and you have not described the person I knew. Even if you were describing him accurately, I don't understand what all of this alcohol business has to do with how he died. Why did you spend so much time on this instead of pursuing the possibility of homicide?"

Sergeant Caple looked back through his notes and the other trooper said, "You have to understand that this report was put together for Mr. Hymes's purposes. This is not a normal investigation report."

"I don't know what to say to that," I said. "Why would Mr. Hymes's purposes be anything other than finding out what happened to this young man, and why would he need anything other than a normal investigation report?"

People argued and again the question didn't get answered, and the meeting slowly dragged to an end.

Later, in Sandra's kitchen, I said, "Caple looks like such an honest and sincere person."

She laughed a bitter laugh. "He was gift wrapped," she said, "and he had a ribbon around his forehead. Hymes tied it there."

An article in the *Flier* mentioned the state police claim that Jon had been in a constant state of intoxication between the ages of fifteen and seventeen. When Sandra read it, she was like a wounded tiger guarding her cubs. In only a few days she had gathered about six dozen notarized statements from Jon's friends, coaches, teachers, and past employers, all saying Jon was one of the more admirable people they had ever met. I wrote one myself. No one recalled his ever being intoxicated in school or on the playing field or at work.

One evening after work I dropped off some statements I had typed, and I asked Sandra, "What are you going to do with them?"

"I don't know," she said. "I just know that we have to do it. I'll give them to Jo Glasco to file. When we need them, they'll be there."

"I don't see what it has to do with finding out what happened to Jon," I said.

Sandra gave me a disgusted look. "Sometimes, you don't understand anything."

As Sandra tells it, Jo Glasco called the *Flier* and said she would sue unless the paper gave Sandra as much space as it had given the state police report. I'm pretty sure Glasco didn't really want Sandra talking to the *Flier* or to anyone in the media, but Sandra intended to have her say.

A reporter came to the daycare center and met with Sandra and a group of Jon's friends. The reporter told Sandra that under the circumstances, and given the way things were in the county, there was only so much he could get printed. He would do what he could, though, to write as favorable an article as he could get past his editors. The article was titled BOWIE KIN, FRIENDS SNUB INVESTIGATIONS.

Several stories were not included in the article. Sandra told me three of them. She sat at her kitchen table and explained that these were stories that people who really wanted to know Jon should hear.

When Jon was in high school, he heard that a friend of his, a girl, was telling people she was thinking about killing herself. Jon went to her house and asked her if it was true and she said it was. He sat up all night with her, listening to her and telling her that she shouldn't do it.

Another was that Jon came home one afternoon from high school, pulled an old pair of jeans from his closet, and started cutting slits across the knees with scissors. Sandra came into his bedroom and asked him what in the world he was doing. He told her that some students at school had laughed at another student who had holes in the knees of his blue jeans. Jon said, "I told him that holes in the knees were in style. I said I had several pairs just like that at home and I would wear some tomorrow to show him. I told some of the guys and they said they would do it, too." Jon came home from school the next day laughing about how well it had worked. "All the guys wore blue jeans with holes in the knees. Anybody who asked, we just told them it was the thing."

And there was a Christmas story. One of the youngsters at the daycare center told Jon he didn't expect much of a Christmas because his family couldn't afford it. Jon spent his entire holiday paycheck buying gifts for the kid.

There was a pleading in Sandra's eyes as she told me these stories that hadn't made it into the papers, or into any of the investigation reports. When she had finished, she leaned over the table, looking down and tightly squeezing a rolled copy of the article that had said as much as could be gotten past the editors. If the paper had been glass, her fingers would have bled.

On the Sunday following the grand jury's decision not to indict anyone in Jon's death, the county insert to the *Baltimore Sun* ran a story under the headline HANGING VICTIM'S FAMILY SEEKS JUSTICE DEPARTMENT PROBE. Tina and Jo, the two lawyers, were behind that. They were doing whatever paperwork and making whatever phone calls and pulling whatever strings were required to get the United States Department of Justice to investigate Jon's death. If the county wouldn't conduct a proper investigation, and the state wouldn't, maybe the Department of Justice would.

I was hopeful again.

Chapter Twenty-five

I NEVER SAW MYSELF as investigating Jon's death. Sometimes I learned bits and pieces that I shared, mainly with Sandra because she was usually present for court hearings and such and could decide for her own reasons what to share with investigators and with her attorneys.

Jim was interested, too, of course, but he was the steady one. Sandra and I talked about trials and investigations. Jim and I talked about cars, golf, football, and whether Sandra and I were likely to get ourselves killed.

One afternoon Sandra handed me a scrap of paper with a license number written on it in purple crayon. "This is the license number of the brown pickup that Jon said was following him the week before he died."

"Jon gave this number to you?"

Jon had given the number to her assistant, Anne Beck, Sandra explained. "She gave it to me and I stuffed it away and couldn't find it. The other day it turned up. When I told Detective Rudacille a brown pickup was following Jon, he said that Officer Riemer had gotten rid of his brown pickup, that he didn't drive one anymore. Then someone told me that Riemer's truck was in the shop for repairs, and that he never sold it. I think Rudacille was trying to throw me off, trying to make me believe that it couldn't have been Riemer following Jon."

Riemer had moved to an apartment complex outside Columbia. I drove there and found myself in a huge complex of town houses. There were hundreds of connected dwellings, each with its own front entrance. I drove around until I located Riemer's address. A copper-colored pickup truck sat in the drive. I pulled behind it and took Sandra's scrap of paper from my jacket pocket. The number on the paper matched the license number of the truck.

I drove to Jim and Sandra's and told them. If the Department of Justice got involved, maybe the information would be useful.

Jeff Phipps's mother, Sylvia, came up with the idea for a plaque. The downtown lakefront was being renovated and you could pay twenty-five dollars to have a paver—a thin brick with an inscription on it—inserted in the brick courtyard that opened onto various walkways overlooking the lake. Jane brought home an application. I filled it out and mailed it along with a note requesting that the town pay for a paver that said:

JON
BOWIE

I received a response asking that I appear at a meeting of the Columbia Council to present the request in person. Public speaking made me nervous, but I called the man who had signed the letter and said I would attend the meeting.

Just before the meeting took place, a woman called and told me I didn't have to appear. The council had decided to install the paver, and the town would pay for it. I hung up the phone and asked Jane if she thought they didn't want me to go to the meeting because I was becoming a nuisance.

"I think so," Jane said. "It's easier for them to just put in the paver. People are beginning to wonder if you're a little nuts."

Sandra was convinced that a statement from Lisa House would help persuade the Justice Department to take an interest in Jon's death, so I went to Lisa's parents' house. Lisa's dad told me Lisa didn't have anything to say to me or to anybody else about the Bowie case, and he showed me the door. I went home and called Mama.

"I'll do what I can," Mama said, "but it's not really up to me. All I can do is ask."

The next day Lisa walked into the daycare center and apologized to Sandra for hiding.

"I was scared," Lisa said.

Jane was a notary, and Lisa met me at Jane's office. At Lisa's insistence, I arranged for her to come when no one else was around. I showed her into Jane's office and closed the door so no one could see her. Her story was the same as Sandra had told me.

A very tall man had followed her in a police car and then confronted her in the parking lot of the Oakland Mills Interfaith Center. She was certain the same man called her later and said that if she didn't back off, he would do the same thing to her he had done to Jon Bowie. Lisa also said she had been running into a lot of police officers lately. One parked outside her house on several occasions and just sat in his car. A female officer stopped her several times for no apparent reason, saying she was keeping an eye on her. Lisa also wondered if her phone was tapped. She kept hearing odd sounds on the line.

I wrote it all down on Jane's computer and printed it out. Lisa signed it, Jane notarized it, and I took the notarized statement to Jo Glasco's office.

"How did you get this?" Jo asked me.

"How religious are you?" I asked her. "Not in the ordinary way. I'm not talking about churches and such, but in a real way."

She studied me a moment and said, "Very."

"Then, when this is over, I'll tell you."

It was only natural for Jo to think I had done something myself to get Lisa to come out of hiding and provide a statement. I couldn't think of any way to explain in a professional setting that Mama had taken care of it, so I didn't go into that. Jo asked if I could persuade another woman to come to her office and provide a statement. On the night Jon died, the woman was one of those dining in Clyde's restaurant when Officer Riemer came in, dressed in uniform even though he was off duty, and made a loud show of being there. The restaurant stop was not part of Riemer's official alibi, and Jo wanted it documented. A second woman who supposedly saw Riemer in the restaurant couldn't be a witness because she and her family had died in a small plane crash. A male diner refused to provide a statement; he had a professional reputation around town, he said, and he was afraid of getting involved. This woman was the only remaining person who might provide a statement. I said I would try.

I called Mama.

"How did you get Lisa to come in?"

"It wasn't up to me whether she came in," Mama said. "I don't give God instructions. After I talked with you, I tried to visit her. It was like going to the moon. She was in bed and I could tell that she was very frightened. She's a religious person, so I told her that she didn't know what fear was until she turned her back on something that God wanted her to do. Then I rolled her around in her bed a little. I hope I didn't overdo it. I didn't want to hurt her."

"She seems all right to me."

"Good."

"Could you do it again? I don't mean go to the moon. Just a gentle reminder that someone should give a statement to Sandra's attorney."

"This is pretty tiring," Mama said, "and I have to be honest with you. I'm getting frustrated with it not leading to anything."

"It's important," I said. "Maybe wait a day or two."

Mama agreed somewhat reluctantly. A couple of days later, the witness from Clyde's stopped by Jo Glasco's office and provided a statement.

You don't just drive up to the window at the Department of Justice and order some to go. It takes time, which you might as well spend doing something else. There was a primary election coming up in September, and a general election in November. In past elections I had handed out campaign pamphlets for State Delegate Ginny Thomas. I had also asked friends to consider voting for another friend who was running for a seat on the Board of Education. Otherwise, I had never been actively involved in local politics. Still, getting involved would hold public attention while we waited to see how the cases between Mickey and the police came out, and if the Department of Justice would investigate Jon's death.

One day during lunch I sat down at a computer and cranked out a draft campaign pamphlet. Using clip art, I created a cover that showed two shoeprints standing in front of a ballot box. A small map of the United States hovered over a slot in the box, waiting to fall inside. I titled the pamphlet *Jon Bowie Still Votes*.

A loosely organized group of supporters named ourselves Friends of Jon Bowie. John Hollywood agreed to be the chairman of what we legally had to call a political action committee. Barbara Stewart—in whose home Jon and Mick had often hung out with her son, Sean—agreed to be the treasurer. Alan Zendell was the self-proclaimed public relations director.

The pamphlet listed several candidates that we supported because they had encouraged or assisted us or been recommended in some meaningful way.

A man named Richard Kinlein had been the county state's attorney in the past, and if he won in the primary, he would oppose Bill Hymes in the general election. Alan Zendell and I met with Kinlein in his office, and Kinlein told us about police officers who took twisted pride in falsely charging people, officers who had lied so often in court they were no longer permitted to testify, and officers who took undue advantage of money allocated for undercover drug buys.

"Hymes drives a car confiscated from an alleged drug dealer," Kinlein said. "A car can be a dangerous incentive. If you can find an excuse to arrest someone, the police department keeps the car. There's a police officer who works in the county right now who drives a Mercedes with a ten-thousand-dollar stereo system in it."

There were police officers, he said, who took pride in killing someone and who boasted, using the Mafia term, that they had made their bones.

Alan asked, "Why do you want to be the state's attorney?" and Kinlein smiled devilishly.

"I don't," he said. "If I thought I had any chance of winning, I wouldn't run. I don't think the people running have any particular desire to do a good job. They just want bigger salaries and their pictures in the paper."

"You could win," Alan said.

"No," Kinlein said. "Hymes has the system behind him, and he'll win. The best we can hope for is to get a few thousand votes, and maybe do a little good in the process."

I went home and added Kinlein's name to the pamphlet.

I photocopied so many campaign pamphlets after hours at a friend's office that sometimes the copying machine overheated and had to cool overnight. I gave copies to Sandra and she distributed them among her friends, who made more copies. Soon we had thousands of copies.

The pamphlet was printed on both sides, and each pamphlet had to be folded twice, creating six narrow pages front and back. People held folding parties in their homes. Sandra's husband, Jim, was the best at folding. He could stack and fold almost a dozen sheets of paper at one time without making them look homemade. When Sandra's assistant at the daycare center, Anne Beck, took a stack home to fold, her husband reminded her that he sold office equipment. He brought home an automatic paper folder, and the campaign really began to take off.

By the time the primary came around, people were sticking pamphlets in screen doors and under windshield wipers throughout most of Columbia and Howard County. On the evening of the primary election, Kinlein joined several of us in Jim and Sandra's basement to watch the election results. Kinlein received a surprisingly large number of votes and was eligible for the November election.

Over the next few days, people we didn't know called Sandra or me and said they were running for office. They would support us if they got elected, they said, but they couldn't say it publicly. Most of them we just ignored.

What I remember most about the primary election is an afternoon stop at a hamburger place. Some nights after distributing pamphlets, I was so tired I fell straight into bed without showering. It was a dumb thing to do, and I came down with a nasty case of athlete's foot between the little and next toe of my left foot. I tried various over-the-counter remedies, but it got worse and was beginning to get infected. I was shy about it and mentioned it only to Jane.

One afternoon Sandra and I sat in a local fast food restaurant eating a hamburger and, out of the blue, Sandra said, "Soak your foot in Clorox."

I was startled because I had not told her about the infection, and I said, "What?"

"I don't know why I said that," she said. "It just came out of my mouth. Is there something wrong with your foot?"

I told her about the problem and her face turned pale.

"I prayed for a sign," she said. "I know it's not good to test God, but I was desperate. I prayed that if God wanted me to know what happened to Jon, He would give me a sign."

"Did you ask for anything in particular?"

"I had to know if it was what I asked for," she said apologetically. "I asked if maybe someone I knew could have a minor injury to the left foot. Nothing serious. Just something to let me know."

I sat staring at her for a moment. Then I laughed.

"Damn," I said. "Maybe you should meet my mother."

Chapter Twenty-six

SANDRA WAS TOO EXCITED to sit at the kitchen table. She pushed open the storm door, and I stepped back off the stoop and kept up alongside her as she started down the parking lot toward the school.

"Jo was at the Justice Department," she said. "An attorney there, a woman, had all of the newspaper clippings about Jon on her desk, and a whole file about Jon."

We walked past the backstop and on behind the school.

"We can't talk about it," she said.

"Why not?"

"I don't know. Jo said if word gets out that the Justice Department is interested, they'll just fold their tents and go away."

"That doesn't make sense," I said. "They're either interested or they're not."

"Who knows?" Sandra said. "It's what she told me."

We turned and walked back toward the house. When we were behind the backstop, Sandra stopped and looked at the ground. "This is where they would have laid him that morning."

"I suppose."

"Sometimes I see that night in my mind, and I can almost make out what happened. There was a flashlight, I think, and some sort of crank thing. I see more than one person, but I can't see the faces."

"I told you my mother saw some sort of mechanical device, like a lift."

"Maybe I'm making it up," Sandra said. "Maybe I see it because your mother saw it."

"Maybe."

Attorney Tina Gutierrez decided that Mickey should take a lie detector test, and she scheduled one in her office in Baltimore. When Sandra called and said Jim was having trouble getting off work, and she was afraid of getting lost in Baltimore, I jumped at the opportunity to drive them.

Lie detector tests, Tina had explained, were almost never admissible in court, but they did have advantages, not the least of which was that they got people's attention. Tina hired an expert with a considerable national reputation, a man named Robert A. Brisentine. He was the retired chief of the polygraph division for the U.S. Army Criminal Investigation Command, commonly referred to as CID. He had established and overseen the implementation of nationwide CID polygraph testing standards. In short, he knew his stuff, and legal and law enforcement professionals knew he did. Brisentine was expensive and Sandra worried about the money, but she and Jim came up with it anyway.

Tina's office was located in a spacious, three-story, renovated Victorian town house in Baltimore. We parked in a gravel parking lot off an alley behind the building and took a long, narrow wrought iron staircase up one flight to the rear door. An assistant informed Sandra that Tina had been called to court, but that the polygraph expert knew what to do. We took seats and waited, talking about anything but the upcoming test.

After a half hour, Brisentine came into the waiting room. He was a tall, gray-haired man with an air of calm self-assurance. He extended a hand to Sandra, and when she stood to greet him her head came up only to his lower chest.

"Ms. Keyser," he said in a courteous, mellow tone, "before you give me a check, there is something that you must understand. I am here to determine if this young man is telling the truth. My reputation depends on that. If you want to know the truth, then fine. If you want to hear what you want to hear, then I must suggest that we stop now. Do you understand?"

"I understand," Sandra said.

Brisentine motioned to Mickey, smiled welcomingly, and he and Mickey disappeared down the hall.

Sandra thumbed hurriedly through magazines without reading them. From time to time she got up and paced the waiting room. I finally said, "You're so nervous you're making me nervous. Mickey's telling the truth. Please relax."

"I know," Sandra said. "But those lie detectors can show all kinds of things. Maybe Mickey's nervous and the test can't tell the difference."

"Tina says this man is the best. He should be able to tell the difference."

Mickey finally returned a little red-cheeked and looking mostly at the floor. Brisentine followed with a wide grin on his face. He stepped over to Sandra, who got up from her seat. He extended a hand and Sandra took it, and he said, "Ms. Keyser, this young man is telling the truth."

Brisentine and Sandra talked and I punched Mickey in the arm, and he returned a self-conscious grin. Brisentine left and we walked down the street for hamburgers and fries, and Sandra and I pumped Mickey for details.

"What did you tell him?" I asked.

"I told him the truth," Mickey said in that disarming way he had of getting straight to the point.

"Come on," Sandra said. "Tell us what happened. What questions did he ask you?"

"Only one," Mickey said. "We talked a while. You know, he asked me about the motel and what had happened and I told him. Then he told me I didn't have to take the test if I didn't want to. He said if I did, though, that it would come out like it came out. He said he had his reputation to look out for. I told him I wanted to take it. He put some things on my arm and asked me if the things I had told him about getting hit at the motel and in the police car were true, and I said, 'Yes.' That was it."

Jim Keyser was playing darts with several other postal carriers one evening at Classics Pub. Classics shared the same parking lot as KoKo's combination convenience store and deli, which Chong Ko's family owned and operated. Jim was a quiet man, but at the same time he didn't miss many details. It was not at all unlike him to wander off for a while to get away from whatever hustle and bustle was going on about him and then to simply return and rejoin the group. That evening, he had gone out to his van to sit and smoke a cigarette. He could smoke in the bar, and did, but going out to the van for a quiet, private smoke was the kind of thing he would naturally do.

Jim sat in his van and watched as several men arrived in a black Ford. One of them got out, went into KoKo's, and came back outside accompanied by Chong. The other men got out of the car, and Chong and the men engaged in a long and sometimes animated conversation. Then the men got back in the car and left, and Chong got into his four-wheel-drive red Toyota and drove away.

Jim put two and two together, added the many details he had picked up listening to Sandra go on about the Justice Department, and realized that, at last, the FBI was actively involved. He went back into the bar to call Sandra, but she wasn't home.

Sandra was shopping at a membership warehouse in Laurel, a few miles south of Columbia, and that just happened to be where Chong went after talking to the men from the FBI. Sandra was wandering the aisles when she and Chong spotted each other. He told her in excited whispers that he had just been interviewed by the FBI.

"They told me not to tell anyone," he said, "but as soon as I saw you, I knew I had to tell you."

Sandra promised not to repeat it, and then hurried home to tell Jim. As she rushed into the kitchen, Jim said, "I have something to tell you."

"First, I have to tell you something," Sandra said, and she was practically jumping up and down. "The FBI is investigating. I just talked to Chong Ko and he told me."

"Damn," Jim said. "That's what I was going to tell you."

Chapter Twenty-seven

ANNE BECK, SANDRA'S ASSISTANT at the daycare center, came up with the idea for a fund-raiser. Anne knew that Sandra and Jim's expenses were piling up. Sandra was grateful, and saw the fund-raiser as a way to keep Jon's death in people's minds.

The event was held in the vast loft of The Other Barn, the renovated barn where the meeting with the police had been held soon after Jon's death. We sold tickets and invited several politicians. Some came and others sent literature but didn't show up.

Several hundred people attended. There was food and music, and people danced. We set aside time for the politicians to speak, which made some of the young people angry. They said they wouldn't have come if they had known they would have to listen to speeches.

The fund-raiser brought in several thousand dollars.

Reverend David Rogers was a born activist. Before moving to Columbia, he directed the Criminal Justice Program for the Cincinnati Council of Churches. By the age of thirty-five, he had worked in backstreets, jails, and prisons, and he thought the county needed a civilian review board to monitor the police. He persuaded County Executive Liz Bobo to invite Police Chief Fred Chaney and members of his staff to a meeting in her office to discuss the review board. My name and Alan Zendell's had been in the newspapers, and Rogers called and invited us to accompany him at the meeting.

Rogers didn't know Jon Bowie, but Reverend John Wright knew Rogers as a police chaplain, a local activist, and a counselor, and Wright had asked Rogers to assist with Jon's funeral. Rogers stayed in touch with Sandra after the funeral, and even offered to meet with Mickey at his Wellspring Counseling Services. After I learned from Sandra that Rogers was connected to the police department, and wanted to spend time with Mickey, I had my doubts about him and had been looking for an opportunity to meet him and size him up. I accepted his offer and so did Zendell.

We sat in a couple of loosely formed rows around a conference table in Bobo's office. Reverend Rogers contended that the county needed a review board to monitor the police, and Bobo said she could live with that. Chief Chaney said it could cause problems for the police, but if people wanted it, he could live with it as well.

After the meeting, Rogers decided to lock in Bobo's support. He wrote a letter to the *Flier* saying that he admired her for taking a stand in favor of a review board. A few days later, I got a phone call from a man who was running for a local office. He said he had overheard Bobo tell Hymes at a political gathering that she had said she would support a review board only to keep us quiet. After the election, she intended to come out against it.

Between Jane's choir work, her job as a village manager, and her naturally outgoing personality, she knew a lot of people in New America, including quite a few local politicians. Columbia's population was increasing rapidly, but county politics still included a sizable good-old-boy network of longtime county residents who often saw Columbians as interlopers. I thought Jane had a better chance than I did of finding out whether to take this man's information seriously, and I asked her to learn what she could about him. She made a few phone calls and told me the man had a good reputation among people she trusted, and who told her that he was not likely to lie.

Sandra and I hadn't decided whether to publicly support Liz

Bobo or her opponent Chuck Ecker for county executive. I called Sandra and told her about the phone call and said, "Put the word out. We're supporting Ecker." She said, "It's done." It was too late to add Ecker's name to the pamphlet, but Sandra knew a lot of people and those people knew more, and it made a difference.

Kinlein lost, which was what he wanted, but he got well over twenty thousand votes, losing to Hymes by only about four thousand. I called Kinlein after the election, and he said he was glad he didn't have to figure out what to do about his secretary, who had worked for him for years.

Liz Bobo lost the county executive race by a few hundred votes even though she had been expected to win in a landslide. A newspaper article suggested that the neighborhood where Sandra lived had turned the election.

As Kinlein had hoped, we had shaken things up a bit, and maybe done some good.

We had also kept Jon's story alive.

A week after the election—timing which I did not see as coincidental—the police department charged officers Riemer, Johnson, and Wright with procedural violations in the motel incident. Internal Affairs had manipulated Jon into dropping charges against Officer Wright, and I don't know how Wright got back into the mix, but he was charged. The charges would automatically be appealed to a panel of three police officers appointed by the chief of police. If the panel agreed with the charges, the officers could be suspended, demoted, transferred, terminated, or docked a day's pay.

Mickey said in a related newspaper article that he was surprised that with witnesses, photographs, and a lie detector test, it had taken almost a year for the officers to be charged. Attorney Jo Glasco said it was too soon to celebrate.

Chapter Twenty-eight

CHONG KO CALLED SANDRA during the weekend after Thanksgiving. Earlier that summer Chong had met a girl named Allison at a party. Allison told him about a friend of hers named Courtney who worked for a national weight-loss chain in Chicago. Courtney had been in Columbia on business the day Jon died. The way Chong told the story, Courtney jogged past the backstop at daybreak and saw two men arguing and a third leaning against the backstop. Later that day she saw Jon's picture on television news and recognized him as the person she had seen leaning against the backstop. She called an attorney friend in Chicago, and the attorney told her not to get involved. He said Maryland was so far from Chicago that it could get messy for her, so she finished her business duties and took a plane back to Chicago. Before leaving, she told her friend Allison what she had seen.

Sandra asked Chong why he had waited so long to tell her, and he said the FBI had told him not to talk about it. He had decided to wait until Thanksgiving to give the FBI time to do something about Jon's death. If they hadn't taken care of it by then, he had made up his mind to tell Sandra.

Chong didn't know Allison or how to locate her, but he remembered the directions to the apartment where she had lived until recently. The next day, Sandra and I followed Chong's directions and found the apartment, and Sandra wrote the address on a scrap of paper.

"Now we give this to Jo to give to the FBI," I said.

Sandra, though, wanted to find out more about Allison.

"What's the point?" I said. "The FBI probably doesn't even need this address. There can't be that many people named Courtney who work for that chain of stores in Chicago. Let the FBI handle it."

We drove away feeling optimistic. If it checked out, we had the promise of an eyewitness who could place Jon with other people at the backstop. The FBI could put two and two together and realize they weren't dealing with a suicide.

Sandra said, "I have a feeling that eventually we'll have to go to Chicago ourselves to find Courtney."

"Why would we do that?"

"I don't know," she said. "The thought just came into my head."

"That's crazy," I said. "You and me going to Chicago? That's nuts."

The police department charged Jeff Phipps with filing a false report for saying he had been strangled at the backstop. They said Jeff made up the story so he wouldn't have to testify in Mickey's trial, despite the fact that Jeff had showed up in court to testify that day after leaving the hospital. He had even been seen on the television news that night standing in front of the courthouse, waiting to testify.

Several months earlier Jeff's mother, Sylvia, told me that Jeff had been subpoenaed to appear in court for filing a false report, but the charge had been dropped. She went to the courthouse and asked to see the book where such charges are listed, and the page for names that begin with the letter P had been torn out. Jeff's attorney called a county attorney in the state's attorney office and asked what was going on. The county attorney admitted during the call that the charge had been made and then dropped, and added, "But we'll get him on something."

As it turned out, that something was the same charge of filing a false report.

Chuck Ecker, the new county executive, fired Chief Chaney. Ecker said they had different managerial styles. Chaney said the firing was political.

Ecker appointed Alan Zendell to a committee that would screen applicants and recommend a new chief of police. Zendell had interviewed political candidates, passed out pamphlets, spoken effectively with reporters, and attended various hearings and other gatherings. Ecker appointed Reverend Rogers and me to a committee that would review the police department.

The committee selecting the new chief got under way first. They met once a week to examine applications and interview candidates, and Alan and I spoke regularly on the phone. One evening a fairly high-level official in the county government phoned me to say that a police major named Jim Robey had applied for the position but should not be considered. I asked for specifics and couldn't extract any.

I passed this information on to Zendell, who agreed to ask Robey pointed questions so he could gauge the man's suitability for the job. I reminded Zendell that when Richard Kinlein was running against Bill Hymes for the county state's attorney, I had asked Kinlein if he knew at least one county police officer that we could trust unequivocally. Without hesitation, Kinlein had named Jim Robey. So, we were getting mixed messages.

After the committee interviewed Robey, Zendell called and said Robey had impressed him immensely. "He's a tough and compassionate man," Zendell said. "He almost had me in tears, and you know how likely that is for me. I asked him if there was anything about his police career that he would change. He told how he once shot and killed a man who had taken a hostage. He actually had tears in his eyes when he talked about it, and I almost did myself."

The time came for the committee to make a recommendation, and Zendell called again.

"It looks like Robey's got the inside track. I could derail it if I wanted. People on the committee are looking to me because of the Bowie thing. Call this person you told me about and see what you can learn."

I called the person and said, "Give me some specifics. I can't go after somebody without a reason."

I hung up and continued sitting at the kitchen table, lost in thought. Jane came in the room, and I vented my frustrations. "Who the hell do people think I am that I should have some say in who becomes the chief of police? What do I know about what it takes to be a good chief of police? I just want to know what happened to Jon, and all this other stuff keeps coming up." Jane kissed me on the forehead and went upstairs.

The person called back a half hour later and said, "That's all you get. My sources won't provide details. They just tell me not to trust Robey."

I thanked him and hung up. Then I called Zendell back. "If you think Robey would make a good chief, then vote for him."

Newspapers announced Robey's appointment a few days later.

The committee charged with reviewing the police department met in a conference room in a county office building in Ellicott City. Twenty-six committee members sat in folding chairs crammed around several large folding tables pushed together. To start the meeting, we went around the table introducing ourselves. There were a half dozen present or retired law enforcement officers, a handful of attorneys in public and private practice, a few teachers, preachers and social workers, and a couple of high school students. One of the attorneys was the assistant state's attorney who had questioned Mickey, Sandra, and others during the county grand jury investigation. It was well known behind the scenes that Jo Glasco would soon be filing a civil lawsuit on Mickey's behalf against the county, and the attorney who would be defending the county in the civil suit was also a committee member.

Call me a pessimist.

The chairperson asked if anyone had anything to say, and a short bulldog of a man, a retired military police officer, leaned forward on his elbows and glared at me across the table. "If anyone on this committee tries to say anything bad about the police, he'll have to answer to me."

I silently vowed to attend all the meetings. My presence might help keep Jon's death in the public eye while we waited to hear from the FBI, but I didn't expect anything I cared about to come of the meetings. What was I going to suggest? That police officers shouldn't hit people without cause, or refuse to investigate homicides? There were already policies in place for that. And I certainly wasn't about to divulge information in the presence of a man who had helped steamroll the grand jury investigation, or the woman who would be defending the county against Mickey's lawsuit.

The committee was called the Citizens Advisory Council for Public Safety, but given the makeup of the committee, I privately labeled it the whitewash committee.

We met every Wednesday and talked, wrote reports, and brought in speakers. Jim Robey, the new chief of police, attended most meetings in uniform to observe. He was a dark-haired, heavyset athletic man of medium height in his forties, with a firm and likable manner. Even members who didn't work for him spoke carefully around him, apologizing for any upcoming remark that might be taken as even mildly critical.

As for the meetings, they brought to mind a fellow I once knew who could sleep sitting up with his eyes open. A reporter called me at home one night after a particularly mind-numbing meeting and asked for my opinion of the committee. I should have taken a beat before speaking, but I didn't. I said, "The whole process could be shortened considerably if we would just get ourselves some little short skirts and pom poms, meet in the center of town, and lead the whole goddamned county in a cheer." He more or less quoted me.

Chapter Twenty-nine

JIM AND SANDRA'S CURLY BLACK TERRIER, Henry, came yipping into the bedroom around two o'clock one morning, tugging at the bed covers and darting back and forth between the door and the foot of the bed. Sandra couldn't quiet him and she finally got up, pulled on a housecoat, and followed him downstairs into the living room. When she was a few steps from the sliding glass door that led onto their rear patio, a dog outside let out a sharp yelp. Sandra flipped on the patio light with one hand and, simultaneously with the other, raised a few rows of blinds.

A tall white man or very light-skinned black man had climbed halfway over their five-foot privacy fence at the rear of the small backyard. Sandra froze, and for a moment, the man froze, staring at the door with his chest pressed against the top of the fence. Then he pushed himself backward and dropped out of sight. Someone behind the fence shouted something in a coarse whisper. Then the running, shuffling footsteps of at least two people hurried away and disappeared behind the row of town houses.

Jim came downstairs, found a flashlight, and went outside to investigate. When he returned, Sandra said she wanted all the windows screwed shut and safety bars installed on the sliding glass door. He promised to take care of it. They finally went back upstairs to the bedroom, but Sandra couldn't sleep. She sat on the edge of the bed, staring out the bedroom window onto the parking lot.

In the wee hours of the morning, the paper carrier parked his economy-size pickup truck and got out. Jeff Phipps's black Doberman, Max, snarled at the paper carrier and cornered him against the front of a town house across the parking lot. The paper carrier screamed for someone to come get the dog, and Jeff came running barefoot out his front door shouting, "What have you done to my dog?" The paper carrier shouted, "I didn't touch him. Get him away from me."

Jeff grabbed up Max in his arms and hurried back inside with blood from the dog streaming down his clothes. Soon afterward, Jeff came back outside carrying Max. He shoved the dog onto the front seat of his car and drove away.

The next evening, I stopped by Jim and Sandra's on the way to a whitewash committee meeting. As I got out of my car, I noticed that large splotches of blood stained the sidewalk and street in front of their house. I walked past Jeff's car and through the driver's window the dashboard looked as if someone had slaughtered a pig on it. Jim and Sandra came outside, and as we walked Jim pointed out blood trails and splatters that continued around and behind the row of town houses to the rear of their unit. Sandra explained that Jeff had taken Max to a vet.

"Max's throat was cut," she said. "It's a wonder he didn't bleed to death."

We went back around the house and inside into the kitchen and I asked, "Did you call the police?"

"They won't do anything," Sandra said. "What can they do?"

"Still, I think you should call them. With everything else that's going on, it needs to be on the record that somebody tried to break into your house in the middle of the night when they had to know you were likely to be home."

Sandra said she would think about it.

After the meeting I stopped again at Jim and Sandra's. A police car was parked in front of the house. Sandra answered the door and I followed her inside. Two uniformed officers, a woman and a male sergeant, were seated at the kitchen table. The woman did most of the questioning until Sandra asked the sergeant what he thought had happened.

"I think it's obvious," he said, "that somebody was trying to get into Jeff Phipps's house and you surprised him."

I said, "What? Sandra sees a man climbing over her privacy fence and you think he was after Jeff?"

The sergeant's face reddened and he asked in a sarcastic tone, "What do you think I should do?"

That's a question I hate to hear from professionals.

"I'd go around back and look around before I made up my mind that Ms. Keyser surprised someone climbing over the wrong fence to get to the house next door."

The sergeant muttered to himself as he and the female officer left to go around back. I stomped back and forth saying how the woman seemed pretty sharp but the sergeant had the IQ of a creek pebble.

Sandra said, "They already looked around back before you got here. I think they only went back again because you said to do it. I think they're a little nervous about being here."

I stopped by the next afternoon, and Sandra asked me to talk with her neighbor, Patti, an excitable, quick-talking brunette who was the wife of John Sinelli, the ex–police officer. I walked up the parking lot and knocked on Patti's door, and she came outside onto the sidewalk. Sandra had told her about the attempted break-in, and Patti said that, in the afternoon before the attempted break-in, she had seen a man in a gray, squared-off car driving slowly in front of Sandra's town house. He was white, dark-haired, and tall. He turned into the parking lot, drove down to the evergreens, and turned around. Patti was in the living room doing her ironing, and she watched through a window as he drove slowly back up the street and stopped in front of Sandra's town house. He sat looking at Sandra's front door, raised an arm to look at his watch, and pulled slowly away.

Patti used her hands when she talked, and when she told me about the man raising his arm to check his watch, she mimicked the motion.

"So, he was left-handed?" Patti gave me a confused look, and I said, "You raised your right arm. Is that what he did?"

She thought about it and raised her hand a few more times. "It was this hand," she said, looking at her right hand.

"I would think a left-handed person would wear his watch on his right arm."

After I left, Patti called the police, and a day or two later two investigators visited her. She told them she was pretty certain she could identify the driver. They escorted her to the police department so she could give a description to a police artist. As they entered the police department, she saw the man she had come to describe sitting at the front desk in a police officer's uniform. She panicked and gave the artist a slightly varied picture, with the nose a little too large and a few other variations.

When Patti returned home, she told her husband that she had seen the man at the police department and had deliberately misled the police artist. John suggested that she ask the investigators to visit them again at their home.

The two investigators returned, and Patti told them she had become frightened and the picture was not accurate. The investigators recorded their conversation with Patti, and at John's insistence Patti made her own recording.

"You don't need a picture," Patti said. "The man I saw was sitting at the front desk when we went into the police department."

One investigator said, "You mean Victor Riemer."

"I don't know," Patti said. "All I know is that the man sitting at the front desk was the man I saw in front of Sandra's house."

The investigators agreed that she had identified Officer Riemer.

Despite the fact that the police knew the sketch was inaccurate, they circulated a flier with the sketch along with photocopied images of several squared-off cars and a request for anyone who had seen the man to call the police department. No one came forward.

Investigators from Internal Affairs also interviewed Patti, and after a few weeks they returned and told Patti it was possible Officer Riemer had been the man she saw but they couldn't do anything about it. Sandra lived on a public street, the investigators explained, and Officer Riemer had a legal right to drive there. It's a free country.

After Jon died, when someone broke into the house, Jim had replaced the front door lock and he put a lock on the gate for the backyard privacy fence. A friend set up a security alarm and ran thread around the gate lock so the alarm would go off if anyone tried to open the gate.

Following the break-in attempt, Jim put special locks on all the doors and windows. He put a safety bar on the rear sliding door in the living room and drilled a hole in the door frame and stuck a nail in it so the door couldn't be opened without first removing the nail. A friend explained how, with string, you could tie an empty coffee can to a doorknob or window latch, and in the can you put a large handful of pennies. If anyone tried to open the door or window, the string toppled the can with a racket equivalent to dropping a tray of spoons on a marble library floor.

Sandra bought a pistol, a .22 caliber Saturday night special. She said she was from West Virginia and she knew how to handle guns. Jim hid the pistol a few times, but she kept finding it and scolding him, and he finally resigned himself to maybe getting hit by a ricochet in his sleep. To anyone who phoned, Sandra made a point of talking about the pistol in case anyone was listening. On the phone, she said what she had bought was an Uzi and that she imagined it would make a good-size hole in the front door from the other end of the hall. She didn't know what an Uzi was, but it sounded frightening so she said it.

From time to time there were reasons for police officers to stop by and ask questions, and two police cars showed up one day in front of the house and the officers got out. Sandra watched and listened through the kitchen window as they argued about who would knock on the front door. "I'm not knocking on that door," one said. "That woman is crazy." They got back in their cars and left.

A sizable group of family, friends, and relatives started watching the house on a regular basis from nine in the evening until sunup. I, several of Jon and Mick's friends, Jim, John Hollywood, Jim's son Mike, and others sat through freezing cold nights. We rotated three shifts a night, sitting in strategically located cars and Jim's van. We wore two and three layers of heavy clothing and brought blankets, sleeping bags, and hot coffee. Sometimes it was so cold we had to crank the engines to warm the cars for a few minutes, which pretty well announced our presence, but it was that cold.

I wasn't aware that anyone involved talked publicly about these nightly watches, but someone must have. A female reporter standing outside the county office building one night after a meeting of the whitewash committee asked me if we were watching the house. Since the objective was to keep anyone away who didn't belong there, I confessed that we were. The newspapers never mentioned our nightly stakeouts, but reporters talk to lots of people, so it was likely that word of the stakeouts got around.

Chapter Thirty

IT WOULD TAKE A LOT to convince me that Lisa House acted on her own. Lisa went to the same church as Sandra, and she had told Sandra the church choir would sing the year before at the July 4 vigil. When the choir didn't show up, she led the gathering in a prayer. Later that same night, the night Jeff Phipps said he was strangled at the backstop, Lisa showed up on Sandra's doorstep saying she had seen a tall man and a smaller man grab Mickey at the backstop. During the grand jury recess, Lisa told Sandra that a tall man followed her in a police car, and later that day she said she was sure she received a threatening phone call from the same man. Then she disappeared and I asked Mama to get her to surface and provide a statement.

One day in Jo Glasco's waiting room, Sandra overheard Glasco tell her secretary that the FBI agent in charge of investigating Jon's death was named Arthur Bellinger. Sandra found an envelope and pencil in her purse and wrote down the name. On several occasions after that Sandra and Lisa and their minister met in the minister's office and prayed for this Arthur Bellinger.

Then, one February afternoon, Sandra answered a knock on her front door and Lisa House was standing there. She was holding two brown grocery sacks filled with clothes and Sunday school teacher's guides.

"Riemer is threatening me," Lisa told Sandra. "I'm afraid to go home."

Sandra took Lisa in. Officer Riemer, Lisa told Sandra, had been calling her regularly, threatening to do terrible sexual things if Lisa testified about seeing two men at the backstop on the night Jeff Phipps said he had been strangled. Lisa said the FBI contacted her and she told them her story.

The FBI knew, Lisa said, that she was coming to live with Sandra. They had, in fact, encouraged it. At the time, neither Sandra nor anyone in her family had been contacted by the FBI, and Sandra still wasn't sure if she was supposed to know the FBI was investigating. To have this supposed link with the investigation show up on her doorstep made her ecstatic.

Sandra prepared the sleeper sofa in the basement and offered Lisa the run of the house. At night, Lisa and Sandra sat up late talking about Jon's death, about the motel incident, and about what Lisa said were her almost daily visits to the FBI offices. Lisa stayed with Sandra and her family until well into the spring, and her behavior was, to put it mildly, suspicious.

In hindsight, it was odd not to think that if the FBI wanted to know something, they would just knock on the door and ask. But Sandra was still a grieving mother, desperate for hope, and she didn't question Lisa's motives for quite a long time. Jim was glad, at first, that Sandra was preoccupied by something other than grief and desperation.

Lisa insisted that the FBI wanted Sandra to get rid of all of the cans and other noise-making contraptions put up to impede an intruder. "If Riemer finds out I'm here and he comes after me," Lisa said, "the FBI might have to come rushing into your house in the middle of the night. They don't want to be stumbling over a bunch of cans." So Sandra removed some, but not all, of those protections. Lisa also told Sandra, "The FBI wants Dave Parrish and his friends to stop watching the house. The FBI says that they're amateurs, and they could complicate things." So we gradually ceased our nightly watches.

The FBI, Lisa claimed, had people all over the neighborhood. She wasn't really supposed to tell, she said, but the FBI had agents staked out in a town house that was for sale across the parking lot, and in a rental unit that overlooked Jim and Sandra's backyard. FBI agents supposedly patrolled the area in two Columbia cabs and a red maintenance truck.

Lisa arranged a meeting, purportedly at the FBI's request, with many of the young people who had been at the Red Roof Inn the previous January. They gathered in Jim and Sandra's basement and she recorded the session. She pumped the kids for details about the motel incident. Who sat where? Who saw what? Who had actually seen Jon and Mickey being hit?

Mickey didn't attend the basement gathering. He found somewhere else to go. He had already had enough of Lisa, and of the FBI, which had not believed him or Jon when they said they had been beaten by police officers. Friends who attended the gathering told Mickey later that Lisa was a nut case, and Mickey said that he always knew that. He could see, he said, that Jim and I went along because we wanted to support Sandra. He figured our support was good for his mother, so at the time he kept his thoughts to himself.

It was Jim who first mentioned that Lisa never seemed tired. He told Sandra, "I think she's sleeping all day and keeping us up all night. And if the FBI wants to know something, why don't they just come ask us? What's all the secrecy about?"

As winter trudged toward March and the promise of spring, Lisa told Sandra the FBI wanted to set up a sting operation. They wanted Lisa and Mickey to take walks at the same time every evening down to the field and past the backstop. The theory was that people who wanted to get to Mickey couldn't because he was always accompanied by other people. If Mickey and Lisa took a walk each evening, word would get out. These people who wanted to get to Mickey might go after him during one of these walks. The FBI, Lisa said, would be watching from various vantage points on and around the school. If anyone tried anything, agents would move in quickly to prevent any harm and to apprehend the culprits.

Sandra fell for the idea because Lisa said the FBI wanted it. Jim and I went along because Sandra wanted it. Mickey said, "That's nuts. I'm not going to parade around down there at night like some sort of target. If the FBI wants me to do that, they can ask me themselves."

It upset Lisa that Mickey wouldn't cooperate. She said the FBI couldn't be publicly associated with Sandra and her family for political reasons, and that it was Officer Riemer the FBI was after.

"No way," Mickey said. "It's crazy."

Mike Keyser, Jim's youngest son by his first marriage, lived nearby and he agreed to stand in for Mickey. The first evening walk took place in early March. Every evening for close to two weeks Mike came to Jim and Sandra's after dinner when it was dark. He pulled a baseball cap down low over his face and dressed in a red and white sweat suit that belonged to Mickey. Mike was a little taller than Mickey, so he slumped a bit to shorten his height when they walked down to the ball field. He carried a loaded .22 pistol in a sweat suit pocket. Lisa told him the FBI said he couldn't do that, and he said, "Like hell I can't. If you want me, you get the gun."

Each night after they returned from their walks, Lisa reported the regular appearances of a gold Toyota and a brown pickup truck. She said the FBI had told her to watch for them. The FBI, she said, ran the license plates for these vehicles and confirmed that they belonged to Riemer and his buddies.

Mike, though, always said afterward that he didn't see any vehicles, and he didn't see the FBI agents Lisa said she saw stationed on top of the school and in cars and behind trees in various locations. Lisa said Mike wasn't very observant.

The walks were into their second week when Mickey came into the kitchen one evening wearing the sweat suit and cap Mike had been wearing. Mike followed him into the room and held out the pistol.

"Nah," Mickey said. "I might shoot myself. I just hope to hell Riemer or whoever's down there does come after me."

When Mickey and Lisa had returned from their walk and he and Sandra were alone in the kitchen, Mickey said, "Mom, she's crazy. There's nobody down there. Lisa keeps pointing here and there and saying, 'See? See?' and there's nothing to see. Mom, she's making it all up."

Sandra confronted Lisa, and Lisa insisted that the FBI wanted the walks to continue, but Mickey's walk was the last. Lisa argued that Sandra didn't appreciate what she was trying to do, that the walks would have worked if they had just kept at it. The FBI was very angry with Sandra, Lisa said, but they would think of another way to get Officer Riemer, because they were convinced Riemer had something to do with Jon's death, and it was their job to prove it.

Lisa said.

According to Lisa, the FBI tapped the phone at her condo. Officer Riemer supposedly kept calling and leaving threatening messages on her answering machine, saying he was going to kill her. When Sandra told me this, I said, "That would make Riemer the stupidest person who ever put on a uniform."

Lisa stuck with her stories, though. She claimed that she stopped by her condo one evening to check her mail and found a box of prophylactics on her porch. Riemer supposedly left a phone message saying he was going to rape her before he killed her.

Lisa started tearing Sandra down. Newspapers reported that Jo Glasco had filed a lawsuit on Mickey's behalf against the county for a little over1.6 million dollars, and Lisa said Sandra was just after the money. Lisa said any money that came from the suit was "devil money" and should be donated to their church.

Sandra finally decided that Lisa had to go. One evening as Sandra began telling Lisa that she had to find another place to stay, a phone call interrupted the conversation. Lisa's sister had supposedly stopped by Lisa's condo to check the mail, and while she was there, she answered the phone. It was Officer Riemer,

Lisa told Sandra excitedly, and he thought Lisa's sister was Lisa and he said he was nearby and was going to kill her. Lisa hurriedly left Jim and Sandra's and drove away.

A half hour later, Lisa called Sandra from her condo and told her that as she left Sandra's neighborhood, she heard sirens and police cars taking off all around. Sandra called me and she was practically screaming. "There were tires squealing and sirens all over the neighborhood." She kept repeating, "They're going to arrest Riemer! They're going to arrest Riemer!"

As it turned out, Sandra hadn't heard police cars and sirens herself. She just believed Lisa. Officer Riemer was not arrested. Lisa returned to Sandra's later that night saying that when she got to her condo, the FBI was already there and the place had been ransacked. Her sister had been too frightened to stay, and whoever ransacked her house had left. The FBI couldn't arrest Riemer because they hadn't actually seen him do anything, Lisa said. They hadn't been monitoring her phone line at that particular time, so they had no evidence. If only her sister hadn't answered the phone, Lisa said, all of it would have been recorded.

Sandra kicked Lisa out.

Chapter Thirty-one

AS SPRING APPROACHED, Jane called me at work one afternoon and said an FBI agent had called and wanted me to call him back. I was immediately nervous. I'd never knowingly spoken to an FBI agent, and mental images of Eliot Ness and J. Edgar Hoover made my heart beat a little faster.

I called the number Jane gave me, and the agent who answered said he had a subpoena for me to appear before a federal grand jury that was considering the Bowie case. The agent lived in Howard County and could drop off the subpoena after work. I said he didn't have to make deliveries on my account. If a grand jury wanted to talk to me, then he could tell me when and where and I'd be there. He insisted, so I told him the earliest I could get home was six.

As I turned onto our side street, I saw the agent's plain black Ford parked in front of the house and my heart started pounding again. He was sitting at the dining room table sipping coffee Jane made for him, and he stood to greet me. He had an appealing combination of firmness and weary warmth about him, and I was relieved that my fantasies born of hero worship had manifested as a normal person.

I sat across the dining room table and he explained the subpoena. He didn't seem to be directly involved in the investigation, and when he asked for a few details I sensed it was more out of courtesy than investigative need. I related in summary fashion what had happened, and told him how I knew Jon.

He gathered papers into his briefcase and we stood. He appeared about to make some polite parting remark but, instead, he said, "I hope you get these Howard County bastards. They beat up my son, too, and there was nothing I could do about it."

When FBI agent Arthur Bellinger called me at work, I was immediately nervous. Still, he had a mild, courteous voice, and he merely asked if we could meet to talk on a certain date, and I said that, since he was with the FBI, any date he wanted was all right.

"You need to understand, Mr. Parrish," he said, "that the FBI is only investigating whether any law enforcement officer was involved in Jon Bowie's death. We're not investigating the motel incident, and we're not investigating whether anyone other than a police officer might have been involved in Jon Bowie's death. If we learn anything that implicates anyone other than a law enforcement officer, we'll turn the information over to the local police."

"I understand," I said.

It was, in fact, something I had not understood until that moment, and I didn't mention my disappointment. If the local police were determined to demonstrate that Jon committed suicide, and the FBI was only interested in whether a police officer killed Jon, there might be no one left to figure out what actually happened.

The FBI office was in a light-industrial area on the outskirts of Baltimore, only a few miles north of Columbia. The one-story building looked like a large, pebble-sided, windowless warehouse. I walked across the graveled lot, clenching my fist in my pants pocket so my palm would be warm and dry when it was time for handshaking.

I was puzzled to see Lisa House's white Mercury Cougar sitting in the parking lot. The license plate had a memorable letter combination, and I was certain it was her car. I walked on as if I hadn't seen it.

A small sign by the front door instructed me to press a buzzer.
A woman's voice asked for my name, and the lock clicked and I
went inside. A polite woman behind a glass partition directed me
to a long row of green vinyl chairs. I sat for a half hour pretend-
ing to read a magazine.

Bellinger entered the room through a heavy door with a security-
code lock. He was a tall, trim, slow-moving man in his early fifties.
With a weary smile, he offered a large hand.

He led me through a gymnasium-size room filled with rows of
mostly unoccupied desks and into a conference room. Chairs up-
holstered with blue leather surrounded the largest walnut conference table I'd ever seen. Bellinger excused himself, apologizing
that he had to attend to other business. I assumed that the other
business had to do with Lisa's car in the parking lot.

I waited, wondering if the room was bugged or if hidden cam-
eras peered through the eyes of portraits on the walls. After a half
hour Bellinger returned, accompanied by a young attorney from
the Department of Justice. The attorney said that he and Bellinger
would have some questions later, but first they wanted to hear
anything I had to say.

One benefit that came of the whitewash committee was that I
had gotten to know Reverend David Rogers better. Rogers and
Sandra and I had spent the previous evening in my basement family room typing a list of about three dozen things we wanted to
make sure the FBI knew about.

"That'll take a while," I said.

"We've got time," the attorney said.

I gave Bellinger and the attorney each a copy of the list and
started at the top. As I went down the list, Bellinger penciled
notes on a yellow legal pad.

A retired law enforcement officer on the whitewash committee
had told me he'd had considerable dealings with the FBI. He said
that if the FBI was serious about a case, they took their notes in
hardbound notebooks. If they weren't serious, they used yellow
legal pads and tossed the notes out later.

I didn't get past the first page of the list, and the little we covered took a couple of hours. I told everything I knew about Jeff Phipps and how the county seemed to be after him for saying he'd been strangled. I went into detail about Jon's house being broken into and his camera and the recorded messages on his answering machine turning up missing. I mentioned an acquaintance of Jon's who lived across town and was rumored to be heavily into drugs, and who had found his truck ransacked the morning Jon was found dead. It was the kind of thing that could mean nothing, but if I was investigating the case, I would want to know about it.

I talked about the threats people were supposed to have gotten during the grand jury. There were those Jeff got, and I mentioned a young witness who had received a threatening call after his name was put on a list of potential grand jury witnesses. I called him by name and said, "You already know about him."

Bellinger looked up from his yellow pad. "Now, tell me who he is again?"

"You must remember," I said, feeling a little frustrated. "A man called him and said, 'If you know what's good for your black ass, you won't testify.'"

When I said "black ass," Bellinger flinched noticeably. There's something disconcerting about seeing an FBI agent flinch, even at a racial slur, and I said apologetically, "It's what was said."

I was pretty worn down from talking so much, and I asked if I could go outside for a cigarette. Bellinger showed me out, and Lisa's white Mercury was still in the parking lot. I smoked the cigarette, went back inside, and Bellinger escorted me back into the conference room. The attorney said he had a few questions for me. It was my first opportunity to get a sense of his and Bellinger's thinking, and I said, "Sure."

"Tell me, Mr. Parrish," he said, "is there anything in your background that would give you reason to have a vendetta against the police?"

After all I had said about the few items on the list we had gotten to so far, it wasn't the first question I expected to come out of his mouth. A red flag went up in my mind, and I said, "No." He sat a few moments looking at me as if he thought I might have more to add, but I didn't. Bellinger finally broke the silence with his own first question.

"We've received a lot of statements that you prepared, and your wife notarized. How do you explain that?" Another red flag went up, but I tried not to show any particular emotion as I answered him.

"That's easy," I said. "Somebody had to do it. I have a computer and my wife is a notary. Some people were pretty nervous about providing statements, and using my wife to notarize the statements made it easy to ensure confidentiality."

Bellinger cleared his throat and doodled on his yellow pad. Then he looked back up. "What is your relationship with Sandra Keyser?"

That was three red flags in a row. I didn't want to get side-tracked, and I ignored the suggestive nature of the question.

"I coached her son in baseball since he was eleven years old, and now he's dead. She's a friend of mine."

Bellinger doodled some more. "What do you think about Lisa House?"

This seemed like a more relevant question, and I said what had been on my mind for some time.

"I figure she's either terrified, emotionally disturbed, or a plant."

When I said "plant," Bellinger flinched again, and his face blanched. He looked legitimately startled.

"What do you mean by plant?"

"I assume she's been telling you the same things she's been telling Sandra and me. She says that Officer Riemer has been threatening her with terrible things. She's also been pumping Sandra for details about things like the Red Roof Inn. It goes beyond idle interest. I figure that if you guys didn't put her up to living with Sandra, somebody did. It certainly would be interesting to find out who, and why."

They ignored my observation. The attorney said they didn't have any other questions, and he thanked me for coming. I had thought that the question and answer session was only an interlude before getting to the rest of my list, and I said, "But we hardly started on the list. Are we going to pick this up again?"

"We'd be happy to do that," Bellinger said, as if it wasn't particularly important. He got up from his chair and the meeting was over. He led me out, gave me a warm handshake at the front door, and said, "We're very serious about this investigation. We intend to find out what happened to Jon Bowie."

"Good," I said. "That comforts me. So do I."

As I left the building, I noticed that Lisa's white Mercury was still in the parking lot.

I had promised Sandra I would stop by her house after the interview. The trees lining the street into her neighborhood had started to bud, and the weather had turned to light-jacket crisp. We walked down the sidewalk and through the evergreens toward the backstop.

"I don't know," I said. "They hardly asked me anything investigative. They wanted to know if I had a vendetta against the police, why I had prepared so many statements, why Jane notarized them, and what my relationship is with you. Aside from anything I could cram in, that was about it. I was a little disappointed."

"Can we trust them?"

"We have to," I said. "This is the FBI we're talking about, and the United States Department of Justice. Who else is there?"

I told her every detail I could remember. I could tell she was listening for anything that might give her even a small reason for hope. I wished I had more to tell her.

I finally decided to share a thought that was nagging me.

"I just wish I could shake this feeling that, instead of investigating Jon's death, they're investigating us."

Chapter Thirty-two

JEFF PHIPPS WAS TRIED in Howard County District Court for filing a false police report when he said he was strangled at the backstop. Rogers and Sandra and I attended along with several young people and several more of Sandra's friends and neighbors. Mickey didn't attend.

First, the prosecution presented its case against Jeff. Officer Tim Burns, the muscular officer who had responded at the Red Roof Inn, and was the first officer on the scene at the backstop where Jon's body was found, testified that Jeff was hyperventilating and appeared very frightened the night he claimed to have been strangled.

When Burns returned to his seat after testifying, the investigating detective, the one who was supposed to be Jeff's friend, leaned over to Burns and whispered loudly, "Why did you say that?"

Burns leaned back and whispered loudly, "Because it's true."

Before the trial, Jeff's mother had showed me her copy of the charging document. The two investigating detectives believed Jeff claimed to have been strangled because he was afraid of testifying at Mickey's trial the next day. This made no sense because Jeff had showed up ready to testify after returning from the hospital, and had even been televised standing in front of the courthouse before the trial started. The report said Jeff's wounds were superficial and were not consistent with his story. Otherwise, the report included no concrete evidence that Jeff made up the story. The charges were based on the opinions of the two detectives, and the detectives repeated these opinions on the witness stand.

One of the detectives testified that he had tried without success to lift the other detective from behind with a cord the way Jeff claimed to have been lifted. Reverend Rogers leaned over and whispered, "Give me a shoestring and I'll lift both those turkeys two feet off the ground."

A doctor who examined Jeff at the emergency room testified that the injuries did not seem severe enough to fit Jeff's story.

Yvonne Last, the emergency room nurse who told me that Jeff's attorney should subpoena his medical records, did not attend the trial.

The young blond woman, who Chong Ko had said falsely accused him of bringing a pipe to the motel, and who, by this time, was no longer Jeff's girlfriend, testified that Jeff had told her that he killed Jon. That was not what Jeff had said, according to the version that circulated among the young people who knew Jeff.

Although Jeff never took the stand to counter this story, the behind-the-scenes version was that, after he and his girlfriend broke up, Jeff had encountered her and friends of hers at a nightclub in Baltimore. She introduced Jeff to her friends as "the person who killed Jon Bowie," and Jeff said, "Yeah, right," the way a person would say, "Sure," or, "Are you kidding?" The county put Jeff's ex-girlfriend on the witness stand to talk about that, without giving the details of the encounter.

And that, essentially, was the county's case.

For the defense, a friend of Jeff's testified that Jeff showed up terrified at his front door in the middle of the night, prompting Jeff's friend to phone the police.

Sandra testified that Lisa House showed up at her house on the night of July 4, upset and insisting she had just seen someone she thought was Mickey being abducted by two men at the backstop.

Lisa testified that she had seen two men approach a young man who was sitting on a team bench at the backstop. She said she looked away, and when she looked back the two men and the young man were gone. This was not what Lisa had told Sandra and me, that she had seen these two men grab the person she thought was Mickey, but in her testimony, she said she had looked away. This was strikingly similar to Jon's second interview with the Internal Affairs Division, when he was led to say he looked away before a nightstick was pressed against his neck. Neither the county attorneys nor Jeff's attorney pressed Lisa for details.

It's been explained to me that sometimes attorneys don't pull out their big guns until there is an appeal. That way, they get everyone on the other side on record without revealing too much about what they know and plan to do. One of the facts Jeff's attorney didn't use was the video recorded by a Baltimore television station showing Jeff standing in front of the courthouse, ready to testify.

A district court judge heard Jeff's case. When all the witnesses had been heard, the judge excused himself and left to consider the case. After a half hour he returned, sat, and started reading from a stack of notes. There was little indication what his decision would be until he finally said, "This case is so bizarre that I feel I have no choice but to believe the police officers."

Jeff was found guilty, and I was stunned, not because I was convinced Jeff was innocent, but because the judge had based his verdict solely on the opinions of two detectives.

Jeff left the room in shock, and his attorney filed for an appeal.

After Jeff's court date, his attorney talked with a writer who lived in Sandra's neighborhood. In the county police report, the writer said he often worked late on his back porch, and he could hear noises from the area of the backstop "crystal clear." He was working late on his porch the night Jon's body was found, and the night Jeff said he was strangled. Jeff's attorney wanted to find out if the writer had heard anything of interest in the early morning hours when Jeff was abducted. He hadn't, but around midnight the night Jon died, he supposedly heard what sounded like young people laughing near the tennis courts, which were beside the school near the backstop. The laughter didn't last long, and he hadn't heard anything else.

By that time I had already seen the police report, and I realized, as the police must have, that the banging and rattling noises that John Sinelli heard around 2:45 a.m. clearly suggested that someone could have made the noises while raising Jon's body onto the backstop. I assumed that the police inserted their version of the writer's statement to counter what Sinelli had said.

Chapter Thirty-three

ON A DAY IN LATE APRIL 1991, I finally confessed to myself that the FBI was not likely to determine what had happened to Jon. I will always think of that day as a numbing day.

Sandra called me at work to say that Attorney Tina Gutierrez had gone to the federal courthouse in Baltimore. Tina was upset because she had sensed that something was amiss, and she wanted to learn what she could. That afternoon when I got home from work, I called her.

"The FBI's doing a tank job," Tina told me.

"A what?"

"You know. This case is going in the tank. The Justice Department has sent a hatchet man from Washington to shut the case down."

"Why?"

"They don't want it investigated."

"What can you do?"

"I can let them know there'll be the devil to pay if they tank this investigation. That should at least drag things out. Maybe something will come up."

I didn't necessarily doubt Agent Bellinger's sincerity, but he worked for the Department of Justice, and if they wanted they could shut down the investigation for whatever reasons they might have. As I hung up the phone, I felt a twinge in the little finger of my right hand, and two fingers and the right side of my hand were immediately numb. The numbness gradually subsided over several months, but even after all these years the finger still has an odd feel about it.

Tina Gutierrez succeeded in getting the federal investigation extended. The federal grand jury that was hearing evidence in the case, she said, probably would end, but the case was still open. I had been subpoenaed but had not been called to testify before the grand jury. I called FBI Agent Bellinger and said I wanted to talk, and we arranged an appointment.

There was a sense of finality to our meeting as I sat facing Bellinger across his desk. I assumed he knew what Tina had told me about the Justice Department trying to halt the investigation, and I didn't see any point in wasting time talking about what had taken place behind the scenes.

We sat in silence a few moments and Bellinger asked, "Do you think Ricmer killed Jon Bowie?"

"I don't know how to answer that," I said. "This is the United States of America, not Nazi Germany. You don't make a charge like that unless you can lay your cards on the table. What I think is not relevant."

"I think Jon died a peaceful death," Bellinger said. "I think he was inebriated and he got into a situation that he couldn't get out of, and he just relaxed and let it happen. Rust on the bottoms of his shoes indicated that he climbed the backstop himself."

I sensed that he was telling me something he wanted me to tell Sandra, regardless of whether he believed it himself. Jon could just as easily have gotten rust on the bottoms of his shoes trying to get off the backstop. I assumed this was also obvious to him, and I let it pass.

"I don't know," I said. "What if someone held a gun on him and told him to climb it? There were those bullets found in the grass."

I couldn't be certain if Bellinger had just forgotten or if he wanted to hear me repeat it in case he might learn something new.

Regardless, I had to go over the bullets again and tell how they were found. It seemed he wasn't really listening so I retold it quickly. When I had finished, he said more to himself than to me, "If we could just get a break. Usually, it takes a break to solve a case like this."

This remark suggested to me that he didn't really think Jon's death was a suicide, that he was just accustomed to holding his cards close to his vest and he was frustrated. I wondered if maybe I had misjudged the FBI investigation, and he had simply done what he could in the time allowed.

"What did you learn about Courtney?" I asked.

"Who?"

"You know, the woman from Chicago who supposedly saw people at the backstop?"

"Our experience is that such things seldom check out," he said. "We can't follow up on every rumor."

I was becoming more adept at continuing a conversation after having been figuratively smacked in the forehead with a shovel, and I kept talking.

"So, if I, say, bumped into her on the street, you wouldn't see it as interfering with the FBI if I stopped and had a chat with her?"

He studied me across the desk and didn't answer.

Sandra took the window seat and I sat in the middle. Two college-age female interns who worked for Reverend Rogers sat together farther back in the plane. Rogers had planned to attend the national conference on police accountability, but a last-minute scheduling conflict prevented him from coming. After arriving in Chicago, we picked up a rental car and drove to the conference, which was held in an old gray stone building that took up most of a city block and looked like a once-elegant bank.

After checking in, we joined a large group discussion. Sandra provided details on Jon's death, and several people from Chicago talked about experiences with the Chicago police that involved boxes with electric wires, plastic bags pulled over people's heads, and leaning people over steam radiators until they confessed to things.

When the discussion was over, a woman named Mary introduced herself to Sandra and me. At Rogers's suggestion, I had called her before leaving Maryland to ask for her help in locating Courtney. Mary said she had found Courtney with one phone call.

"She said it was odd that I called her at that particular time because she had just gotten off the phone with an FBI agent from Baltimore."

Sandra and I exchanged glances and didn't interrupt.

"I don't know if you should go see her," Mary said. "She said that the FBI wants to fly her to Baltimore to testify before a grand jury. The agent told her to call him immediately if anyone connected with the Bowie case contacts her."

"Damn," I said. "The FBI knew about Courtney six months ago. Now they call her a few hours before Sandra and I get off the plane? I really don't understand what's going on here. Will she call the FBI and say she talked with you?"

"I asked her that," Mary said. "She says she won't since I'm not really connected to the case. Besides, she says she doesn't know anything. She says it's all some sort of confusion. When she went past the backstop, the body had already been discovered. The only people she saw were the people taking the body down, and the bystanders."

Surprised and disappointed, I said, "It still aggravates me. All the FBI had to do was call their Chicago office six months ago and find out that she didn't have anything to say. Why fly her to Baltimore now? It's grandstanding. They really do want to kill this investigation."

Mary handed me a slip of paper with Courtney's full name, address, and phone number. "It might not be smart to call her until after she talks with the FBI," she said. "They could say you tried to influence her."

The next morning, Sandra and I ate fast food breakfast sandwiches as I drove and she leaned over a map of Chicago. Courtney lived only a few miles from the conference center in an attractive brick, tree-shaded town house. We drove past a few times and then parked by the curb. I said, "I can't believe we've come all the way to Chicago to talk to this woman, and now we're right in front of her house and can't do it."

"We can't," Sandra said. "It would be used against us somehow."

We returned to the conference center and spent the day with groups from Dallas, Los Angeles, Boston, Minneapolis, New York, you name it. An ex–police officer talked about being drummed out of police work for speaking out against police brutality. Another officer said things had to change—it wasn't enough just to complain. A young Latino woman from Los Angeles talked about the Rodney King case, which still was an evolving story at the time. She didn't think the Justice Department wanted to deal with the King case. People in Los Angeles were trying to apply pressure so the case didn't simply disappear.

Sandra and the interns and I had a fairly early flight, so we left Sunday morning before the conference ended. We didn't talk much on the way home.

Chapter Thirty-four

ON MAY 4, 1991, the first anniversary of Jon's death, a crowd of people attended a vigil at the backstop and held candles around the baseline in remembrance. Reverend Rogers, County Councilman Vernon Gray, and I talked, and Barbara Stewart ended the ceremony with "The Wind Beneath My Wings," accompanied by Reverend Rogers on acoustic guitar.

That spring, the whitewash committee held public hearings. People stood up in front of committee members and said they liked the police or didn't like the police or had experienced some good or bad encounter.

Sandra came to one of the first meetings in the basement of a small rural church. She stood in the audience holding notarized statements from people who reported that, contrary to what the police report said, they had not told the police they had seen Jon climbing the backstop or drinking heavily. Sandra had asked the previous chief to add the statements to the police report, in accordance with the law, but they hadn't been added. The new chief, Robey, was at the meeting, and Sandra handed him the statements and asked him to add them to the police report.

In June 1991, my older son Michael married his high school sweetheart. Reverend David Rogers performed the outdoor ceremony in the luscious backyard garden setting of an elegant, white stucco country estate in the Columbia village of Town Center.

Mama, my dad, and my brothers and their wives came to our home after the wedding for snacks and to catch up on each other's lives. Mama found a discreet moment and asked, "Can you show me some tunnels?"

"I think I've found it," I said.

We slipped out and I drove her to a tunnel that ran under a street about three quarters of a mile from the backstop. An asphalt bike path led through the tunnel and into the woods until it crossed the street near the high school and continued on into Jim and Sandra's neighborhood. We parked on a side street, crossed over, and followed the bike path down a steep slope toward a high embankment where the path turned sharply into the tunnel entrance.

We had taken only a few steps inside the tunnel when Mama stopped and said, "I'm frightened. I'm so frightened. I can feel the hair standing up on the back of my neck."

Her shoulders were drawn tight in fear and she looked at the floor.

"He tried to hide here," she said. "He ran and they chased him, and he came here to hide."

The public still didn't know that the FBI was investigating Jon's death until a newspaper article said that Officer Riemer had been subpoenaed to appear before a federal grand jury. The article created quite a stir in the whitewash committee. On the day the story was published, they talked excitedly before the meeting, asking who had seen the article and what it might mean. With genuine shock and surprise, they asked each other why the FBI would be investigating Jon's death. Since, barring a miracle, I had all but given up hope that the FBI would come up with anything, I didn't join the conversation.

After the meeting, I was standing on the sidewalk smoking a cigarette and Chief Robey walked up to me.

"What's it like," he asked, "being Sandra Keyser's friend?"

Without so much as a preliminary thought, I said, "It's like being the dog that caught the wheel."

Robey let out a belly laugh and, catching an imaginary wheel in his teeth, vigorously shook his head 'round and 'round in a circle.

The county police report said that a young man had told a young woman that Jon often climbed the backstop, horsing around. This is called "seed planting," the purpose being to demonstrate that Jon was familiar with the backstop and might logically have climbed it to commit suicide. Both young people signed notarized statements saying this conversation never took place, and neither had ever known Jon to climb the backstop.

Detective Rudacille says in the police report that another young woman once saw Jon drink two six-packs of beer and get "giddy" from alcohol, but not overly drunk. Rudacille notes parenthetically that getting giddy requires about the same amount of alcohol as Jon would have had before he died. The implication, of course, is that Jon could easily have climbed the backstop after drinking a lot of beer. Rudacille also says that this young woman had heard Jon and his friends brag about climbing the backstop, saying such things as, "I got all the way to the top and you didn't."

Talk about seed planting. I was probably nine or ten years old the first time I climbed a backstop for the fun of it. I got all the way to the top and never gave it a second thought. In the police report, Rudacille is talking about teenagers in high school, some of whom, Jon included, were natural athletes. The young woman to whom this silliness was attributed wrote the chief of police saying that none of the statements attributed to her in the police report were true. She also retained an attorney, who wrote the *Columbia Flier* and suggested that it not include the statements attributed to his client in any articles about the case.

Another officer said in the report that emergency room nurse Yvonne Last had assisted when Jon was treated for various injuries he received in fights "and so on," and she was aware that Jon had taken drugs but was getting better in that regard. She said that she had heard that Jon owed someone money for drugs and his death probably was because someone wanted to make an example for others to see.

Not even close. In addition to working in the local emergency room, Yvonne Last also worked in the local walk-in clinic where Sandra took Jon after he broke his hand hitting a coffee table during the Super Bowl, and when he broke a finger playing baseball. As for drugs, the report says that Yvonne Last heard this from an emergency room coworker. Sandra told me that when Jo Glasco learned this, she contacted the coworker, who was astounded that his name had come up. He said he stood around in a group of people talking about Jon's death the first day it appeared in the newspapers, and they had speculated about what might have happened. The coworker didn't sign a statement. He called the police department and said he wanted the police report amended to remove anything attributed to him. He also wrote the *Columbia Flier* and suggested that they not use his name in any article related to Jon's death. He said that since things attributed to him had gotten so misconstrued, the *Flier* might want to cast a suspicious eye on anything in the police report.

Brian Bumbrey—who had said in newspapers that he had sold drugs for two county police officers—was being held in the maximum-security state penitentiary in Jessup, Maryland, just outside of Columbia. Reverend Rogers pestered the FBI to interview Bumbrey and finally decided that the FBI wasn't interested. Rogers had counseled prisoners, and he decided to interview Bumbrey himself.

I rode with Rogers to the prison one afternoon and waited in the car for over an hour. When he came out, we rode to my house and Rogers sat on the living room sofa thumbing through his penciled notes.

Bumbrey told Rogers that he had been arrested for burglary. A police officer offered to get the charges dropped if Bumbrey would help him sell cocaine that had been confiscated during various arrests. Bumbrey said that he didn't know anything about selling cocaine, and he wasn't selling it fast enough to satisfy the officer

and his officer friends. He didn't know Jon well, but they sometimes attended the same parties at different people's homes. He
approached Jon and asked him to introduce him to friends who
used cocaine. Jon wasn't a user, Bumbrey said, but he knew people who were.

"It sounded like he knew what he was talking about," Rogers
said. "He named kids you and I know, friends of Jon and Mickey's,
and he described them and the places where the parties were held."

"Did he give the officers' names?"

"Yep," Rogers said. He checked his notes and read the names
of three officers I had heard of and two I hadn't. Each, Rogers
said, was either directly involved or knew about the sales. "He
says Jon's death didn't have anything to do with the Red Roof
Inn. That's just a convenient smoke screen that came up. All the
attention took the heat off the people who really did it."

"Who does he say did it?"

"He does a tap dance about that. He says he's sure it was the
police, but he wasn't there."

"But why would the police want to kill Jon if all he did was
give Bumbrey some names?"

"He says Jon hid and photographed him making an illegal exchange with some police officers who were selling drugs. Jon
thought that if he could prove that police officers were selling
drugs, it would somehow add credibility to his and Mickey's
claims that they had been beaten. Bumbrey says the police found
out that Jon had photographed them."

"That could explain the camera that was missing after Jon
died. Do you believe him?"

"Who knows?" Rogers said. "It seems he's holding something
back, being evasive about the extent to which he was directly involved. I suppose there could be some truth in it."

"So, basically, this guy is saying a lot of things, but we don't
have any way to prove it."

"I'll have to talk to him again," Rogers said.

"And the FBI still hasn't talked with him?"

"Not according to him."

"And the county?"

Rogers laughed a cynical laugh. "Two detectives," he said. "They got a release to drive Bumbrey around town and show them locations that he had burglarized. Bumbrey told the guard at the prison that he was afraid to leave with the detectives, and the guard said he had to go. He was terrified. He thought they were going to kill him. The detectives drove him around town, showing him places that he had already told the police about. Then they drove back to the prison and parked. One of the detectives turned to him and said, 'Now, what's this crap about police officers selling drugs?' Bumbrey wasn't about to tell them anything," Rogers said. "He told them to go screw themselves. That was the county investigation."

"So, the FBI won't talk with him, and the county has already done what it calls its investigation. Why is he willing to talk with you? What's in it for him?"

"He says that he feels bad about what happened to Jon, and he feels bad for Jon's mother. He wants to do something about it."

"Goodness of his heart."

"That's what he says."

Reverend Rogers obtained the slides of the West Virginia autopsy from Jo Glasco. I met with him in his office and he turned off the lights, pulled the long, vertical blinds, and flicked on a projector.

"You don't have to do this," he told me.

"I'll be fine," I said. I took a deep breath and reminded myself it was only pictures.

Rogers flipped through the slides and we questioned any unusual marks or bruises. We decided the marks on the stomach and chest could have been caused by the rope that the rescue squad had used to lower Jon from the backstop, and by the backstop wire itself. The marks around the upper neck were clearly caused by the cable.

More slides showed the bruises that were described in the West Virginia autopsy report but not in the Maryland report. One bruise came up the front of Jon's right shoulder from underneath the armpit. The other, the large, horizontal Y-shaped bruise at the lower right side of the neck, was just above the collarbone.

I was surprised that the Y-shaped bruise was so strikingly prominent, and I asked, "What could have caused that?"

"Don't know," Rogers said. "Let's find out." He went to his desk and picked up the phone.

"Who are you calling?"

"The state medical examiner in West Virginia. They're his slides."

He got the medical examiner on the phone, and the two of them had a lengthy conversation. When he hung up, he said, "That bruise worries him, too. He says that, in all likelihood, it was not caused by the cable. It's more likely that it was caused by a single, straight-on blow from some object. You heard me ask if it could have caused death."

Rogers moved a finger down his penciled notes.

"His answer was, 'It was a significant enough injury to have been the cause of death.'"

That night, I had nightmares.

Reverend Rogers arranged a meeting with Chief Robey, and asked Sandra and me to come. The meeting wasn't publicized, but the three of us couldn't walk into the police department without being noticed. Some in the police department would undoubtedly see the meeting as evidence that the new chief didn't support his officers. Robey was a man caught in the middle. He greeted us cordially, and we sat with him and his chief assistant around a small, round table in his office.

Sandra wanted to make sure Robey knew that someone had broken into her home at the same time Jon's body was being lowered from the backstop, and that Jon's camera, house key, and the tape to his answering machine were missing.

Robey apparently hadn't heard these facts, but he brushed them off with, "We probably couldn't have found the person anyway," meaning the intruder.

We talked about whether the snuff can that showed up where Jeff Phipps said he was strangled had any fingerprints on it, why laboratory results showed no rain water on Jon's clothing when it had rained that night, whether the police report could include sworn statements of people who said that the things attributed to them in the report were inaccurate, and on and on.

When the meeting was over, we shook hands. As Robey shook mine, he said, "We will do everything that can be done."

I said, "It leads where it leads."

In the parking lot as we were leaving, I said, "I hope Robey doesn't just check off the things we told him and close the investigation."

"Don't be so cynical," Rogers said.

"I don't trust them," Sandra said. "Nothing's coming of this. It's a waste of time."

Chapter Thirty-five

THE POLICE DEPARTMENT'S Internal Affairs Division found Officers Riemer and Johnson guilty of violating department policies, and of using excessive force. Officer Pete Wright, who had been charged originally, was not charged; I didn't know why. The officers' attorneys appealed the IAD decision to the trial board, and in August 1991, more than a year and a half after the incident at the Red Roof Inn, the board convened.

The hearing lasted for three days, recessed for two months, met again for a day or two, and ended. An attorney from the county Office of Law represented Mickey. The attorney called several of the young people who had been at the motel, including Mickey, and they described in detail what had happened. The attorney also called a police training instructor who testified that no police officer is trained to choke a person or hit a person in the face unless it's a life-threatening situation. The attorney tried to call an investigator from IAD, but the officers running the trial board wouldn't allow it. Other people at the motel had come out of their rooms that night to watch as the police arrested Jon and Mickey, but none of these people were called.

The great majority of the time was spent as Riemer's attorney cross-examined Mickey and the others who had been at the motel, basically trying to make it appear that they were lying. There were no corroborating details or witnesses to counter what the young people said. Just clever questions. The two accused police officers never took the stand. In fact, the only defense witness was Sergeant Caple of the Maryland State Police. Caple's testimony consisted almost entirely of his reading into the record those parts of the state police report that claimed Jon had a drinking problem.

The hearing ended and a few more weeks went by. Sandra kept getting calls telling her to go to this building or that because the board of officers had reached a verdict, and she kept getting called again and told that a decision had been delayed. Finally, in November, the verdict was in. Reporters came and Riemer's and Johnson's and Sandra's friends and families came.

Mickey wouldn't go. He told Sandra, "You know what they're going to decide. I'm not wasting my time."

Officers Johnson and Riemer were found innocent.

Sergeant Caple's testimony at the police trial board included the claims in the state police report about Jon getting into various fights and breaking bones, about Brian Bumbrey, and the claim that Jon was "usually in an intoxicated state." There was no mention of the dozens of people who would have painted a completely different picture of Jon.

Caple never talked to the varsity baseball coach, Jerome Jefferson—J.J. the kids called him. Caple thought he had talked with J.J., but he was talking to the assistant coach, who told Caple he didn't know anything about a drinking problem.

A month before Jon died, a state investigator conducted a routine background investigation and reported that Jon was fit to continue working at the daycare center. Two women who worked for the Maryland human resources department observed the daycare center. From the time Jon was sixteen until he was nineteen, they monitored and approved his classroom performance as an assistant. They gladly would have talked with the state police if they had been asked.

If she could, Sandra would have read into the trial board record all sixty-plus statements that people had written in support of Jon, but these weren't admitted into the record.

Jon's high school homeroom teacher never saw Jon in an inebriated state and asked to be contacted if any further information was needed.

Coach Jefferson wrote that he was shocked anyone would say Jon had a drinking problem because, if he had, Jefferson would have known about it.

Jon's American Legion baseball coach wrote that he'd never noticed any drinking problem, and Jon's recreational league football coach wrote the same.

Parents at the daycare center wrote that they had never seen any indication that Jon had been drinking, and the woman who owned the daycare center wrote, "Why didn't this so-called investigation team talk to anyone who really knew Jon?"

A man who had known Jon for ten years wrote that he had employed Jon one summer to supervise his children forty hours a week, and had used him as a babysitter for years. He never saw any indication of alcohol or drug use.

A special assistant to the Superintendent of Schools in Annapolis, whose children stayed at the daycare school, had welcomed Jon in his home for sleepovers with his son, had used Jon on his softball team, and had never seen Jon under the influence of alcohol or drugs.

Another parent wrote, "Quite personally, I'd like to see an investigation of what happened to Jon Bowie instead of a phony assassination of a fine young man's character."

Neighbors wrote that they had never observed any alcohol or drug use and usually saw Jon and Mickey going to or coming from some athletic event, which was how the twins spent most of their time.

Jon's high school sociology teacher wrote that he was not aware of any alcohol problem, and asked to be contacted if any additional information was required.

I could go on and on. The state police said one thing without revealing where they got their information, and people who knew Jon said something else.

Sergeant Caple didn't testify where he got the information that Jon was usually intoxicated, but he had previously mentioned in a meeting with Sandra and Jo Glasco that his primary source was Officer Tim Burns, Riemer's drinking buddy.

A young high school student on the whitewash committee came up with the idea for a survey to determine if the community was satisfied with the police. Her survey asked such questions as, "Are you happy with the police department?" and "Do you feel safe?" Thousands of copies were included with water bills, and about seventeen hundred came back.

Most survey responses reflected general satisfaction with the police. Some committee members regarded this finding as a major milestone, and the *Columbia Flier* reported it.

A woman who worked at the post office in a community north of Columbia told Sandra that she had been asked to ensure that the survey was mailed to rural zip codes where mostly older people lived. The woman wouldn't say this publicly for fear of losing her job.

Sandra and a friend hit the streets with a petition for a civilian review board to oversee complaints against the police department. They gathered twenty-four hundred signatures in a fairly short time and showed up at a meeting of the whitewash committee to present the petition.

The high school student who designed the committee's study said that Sandra's petition was not valid. Most of the other committee members said nothing, and the committee considered Sandra's petition for under five minutes.

I was not in favor of a review board. I didn't think anything would change how some police officers acted until other officers stopped putting up with it. Still, it irritated me that the committee had laughed off Sandra's petition, and I voted for the review board. By then, so many members had quit the committee in disgust or boredom that the recommendation actually came within a few votes of passing.

Newspaper articles reported that the committee had decided not to recommend a review board. Rogers said in an article in the *Flier* that he wasn't surprised since the committee included so many present or retired police officers. I said that voting for a review board could make it look as if something wrong might have happened at the Red Roof Inn. Other committee members said that Rogers and I were just sore losers.

One afternoon in the early winter of 1991, I stopped by Jim and Sandra's and Sandra pointed to a large manila envelope on her kitchen table. She said it had been laying there for several days. The return address read Department of Police.

"I can't open it," she said. "I know what it says, and I don't want to read it."

I took the envelope home, sat at my kitchen table, and opened it. It contained a three-page letter addressed to Sandra and signed by Chief Robey. Item by item, the letter listed and explained away each of the things Rogers, Sandra, and I had discussed in our meeting with Robey. After reading the first few items, I lowered my head and muttered, "Damn. They settled for public relations and ass covering."

The letter ended by stating that the police department's investigation of "the incident" was concluded.

I waited a few days before stopping by Sandra's again. I laid the envelope on her kitchen table.

"It's what you think."

She flinched, and busied herself by cleaning the kitchen counter.

"Robey closed the case," I said, and she cleaned harder. "From the way it's worded, it wouldn't surprise me if the Office of Law wrote it for him. It's all so careful and precise."

Sandra came to the table and sat, holding her cleaning towel in her lap and squeezing it with both hands. "So, they didn't investigate anything."

It was more of a statement than a question.

"I wouldn't call it an investigation," I said. "They were just touching all the bases. Now, if we ever complain about the investigation, they can say they looked into everything we told them about."

Sandra lifted the rag in front of her face and I thought she was going to strike the table with it, but she lowered her hand and rested it on the table.

"They're all a bunch of crooks," she said.

I'd had a few days to calm down after my own disappointment so, instead of fueling her anger, I said, "No. It's tougher than that. What they are is mostly a bunch of decent people who believe in what they're doing. That's what makes it so hard."

She looked at me as if I'd asked her a riddle that made no sense.

"How can you say that? You almost sound like one of them."

Her saying it stung me some, but I didn't feel like arguing.

"I'm not saying that what they're doing is right. I'm just saying that most of them find it convenient to believe that it is."

A young criminal justice major who worked with Reverend Rogers that winter also worked part-time at another local business establishment. In a conversation with her boss at the other job, it came out that she had an interest in the Bowie case. Her boss went into a shouting tirade and said that he had a personal friend and neighbor who was an FBI agent, and the agent had told him that the FBI was preparing a report that would tear Sandra and her friends up one side and down the other. The young woman mentioned this tirade to Reverend Rogers, who repeated it to Mickey's attorney, Tina Gutierrez.

Soon after, two men knocked on Sandra's door one afternoon and introduced themselves as FBI agents. It seemed that the FBI was doing an internal investigation to determine if agents were leaking information. The conversation quickly turned to Reverend Rogers and his involvement in the Bowie case. Rogers, at that

time, was serving as interim pastor of a small church in Taneytown, an hour northwest of Columbia. One of the agents asked
with total sincerity, "Does Reverend Rogers run a cult?"

Sandra was so taken aback at the absurdity of the question that
she laughed out loud.

"He certainly does," she said, "and it's filled with little purple-
haired ladies from Taneytown. If I were you, I'd drive up there
one Sunday and investigate it."

The FBI eventually concluded that a Howard County police
officer, not an FBI agent, was spreading word that the final FBI
report would tear Sandra and her friends apart.

In the middle of January 1992, two FBI agents hand-delivered a
letter from Linda Davis, the head of the criminal section of the
Civil Rights Division of the United States Department of Justice.
Mickey was home alone, and they handed him the letter and left.
The letter contained only three short paragraphs, and no specifics,
and one sentence in the middle said it all.

After a thorough investigation and careful review of the
evidence we concluded that this matter should be closed.

Several weeks later an article in the *Washington Post* said the
Justice Department had announced that the case was closed. In a
related article, Chief Robey said he was pleased that it was finally over.

Jeff Phipps was sentenced to two years' probation for filing a
false report when he claimed that he had been strangled at the
same backstop where Jon's body was found. Jeff's attorney said
Jeff had pled guilty using what is called an Alford plea. You
agree that you could be found guilty although you still contend
that you are innocent. The judge said the sentence would let Jeff
"get his life together," and Jeff said he just wished the whole
thing would end.

* * *

There was no planned vigil for Jon on May 4, 1992, the second anniversary of his death. A few people went to the backstop, each for private reasons. Some laid flowers at the base of the backstop. Others tied flowers to the backstop or threaded them through the wire.

By then Mickey had transferred to the University of Maryland in College Park. Sandra called him and suggested that he not drive up. She thought it would be too difficult for him, and he was relieved.

Toward evening, when no one else was around, I drove to the school and sat in the car in the parking lot, looking at the ball fields and the backstop.

I didn't stay long.

Reverend David Rogers—as a result of his activism, counseling services, and connections within the criminal justice system—had acquired a wide variety of friends and acquaintances from many walks of life. One afternoon he found himself talking with one particular friend across a back-corner table in a dimly lighted bar.

The friend said, "Could you use a mechanic?"

Confused, Rogers said, "There's nothing wrong with my car."

The friend said, "I wasn't talking about cars. I was talking about the Bowie case. You said you had a problem. Could you use a mechanic?"

Rogers sat looking for a while at his friend as he slowly realized what he was being asked.

"Oh. A mechanic. Is that what it's called?"

"This man, Riemer," the friend said. "We wouldn't put up with that in . . ." and he named a city, a major metropolitan area in another state.

Rogers took a long sip of beer and thought about it. Finally, he said, "No. That wouldn't be right. I can't talk about how wrong this was on the one hand and, on the other, turn around and do the same kind of thing. Besides, maybe Riemer had nothing to do with it. I wouldn't want to make a mistake like that."

"All I'm saying," the friend said, "is that we wouldn't put up with that kind of thing in . . ." and he named the city again.

"No. Thank you, but no. I couldn't go along with that."

They sipped their beers in silence. Then the friend said, "Okay. If that's how you feel about it. Just remember, the offer stands."

They finished their beers and left, each in his own direction.

Chapter Thirty-six

ALL THE INVESTIGATIONS WERE OVER. Only Mickey's civil suit against the county and the pending charges against him in the motel incident remained unresolved.

Reverend Rogers and Sandra and I still held out hope that some clue, some persuasive bit of information, might emerge that would interest the FBI enough to reopen its investigation. Our only remaining option was to venture outside of law enforcement.

Psychics who investigated crimes were not all that common at the time, but they were beginning to appear on television programs and in magazine articles.

I scheduled a telephone appointment with Ms. Noreen Renier, who lived in Florida and made her living as a psychic detective, working primarily with law enforcement agencies. During her readings, Ms. Renier liked to hold clothing or personal objects that belonged to the subject.

The Howard County Police Department still had Jon's clothing from the backstop, so Reverend Rogers, Sandra, and I went together one morning to the police department. Sandra signed for a large, brown cardboard box containing Jon's clothing and other personal items. Taking possession of Jon's effects officially broke the "chain of evidence," meaning that the items in the box were no longer legally viable. Since the investigations had ended, Sandra didn't care. She just didn't want to look inside the box.

A day or two after we picked up the box, an FBI agent phoned Sandra at home, asking what she intended to do with the evidence. Getting the call after the FBI's case was officially closed surprised her, but it also encouraged her. She told the agent where and why she was sending the box in case the FBI might someday reopen their investigation.

In July 1992, Jane joined me in the first conversation with Ms. Renier. On the day of the appointment, I took a long lunch break and drove home. I sat at the kitchen table and used the wall phone. Jane took a kitchen chair upstairs and used the bedroom extension. Two assistants and a professional police artist joined Ms. Renier in her home. All Ms. Renier and those with her knew about Jon was his nickname and that his death had been ruled a suicide in 1990.

In condensed form, because the reading lasted well over two hours, Ms. Renier began by observing that Jon was close to his mother, and he had broken his arm when he was younger. This wasn't quite right—he had broken his hand and a finger—but it was close enough, and I didn't interrupt.

Ms. Renier quickly concluded that Jon's death was a homicide. She said there had to have been more than one person involved because, "The only way anyone could get me to go where I didn't want to go would be to have me unconscious, and carry me out."

I hadn't mentioned autopsies, but Ms. Renier said, "I think the first autopsy really was sloppy. I feel like it went through what was so obvious instead of examining other parts of the body."

The police artist drew as she described the person she felt was responsible for Jon's death. She described a slender man of mixed nationality who stood about five-ten or five-eleven. He had a wiry, muscular build, an obvious Adam's apple, wiry, unparted hair, and was about thirty-two, but looked older.

After describing the man, she said her lower neck hurt on the right side, along the neckline.

"It's just, really killing me," she said.

Her assistant asked if I could confirm the lower neck injury, and I thought of the Y-shaped bruise that was described only in the second autopsy.

"Yes."

Noreen said that Jon was not killed where he was found. She thought the people involved had to know Jon well and were familiar with where he lived.

Jane said that Jon had been at a party that night and then left, and she asked, "Did he meet up with some friends, or did he run into some people going home?"

"I could have picked up somebody there, or given somebody a ride."

I asked, "Could it have been you who was picked up?"

"Oh, yes, yes, yes," she said. She asked if Jon could have been picked up in a truck, and I didn't know. Her assistant asked if Jon was familiar with the other people in the truck.

"He might be from the old neighborhood."

I asked, "How does Jon feel about this person?"

"I'm a little nervous. It seems like we've got some serious business going to go down, and I can feel it. I can feel it. Somebody else is in the back. I feel something going around my neck. Me struggling. Other things happening. I think I was killed in the car."

The switch from truck to car threw me, and I drew a blank.

"I'd like to know more about why these people did that," I said.

"They had to get rid of me. They didn't want it to look like murder, so everybody'd be up at arms and could make the connection. So, it had to look like suicide."

I asked, "Was it premeditated?"

"We knew we were going to do it. I don't know if we knew exactly that time. I think it was premeditated without . . . with maybe a blank in exactly when it was going to go down. It was going to go down."

Noreen's assistant instructed, "Jon wants to relate some clue, some lead. He wants these killers to be found. He wants this matter cleared up—"

Noreen interrupted. "I feel, really, it has to come from some-body that's already in prison."

Thinking of Brian Bumbrey, I said, "We might know some-thing about that."

I asked her to describe the person in prison and she said he might wear glasses, and he looked young. He had a very distinct Southern accent and might be studying or in some way be in-volved in schooling.

Jane asked, "Do you feel that this person in prison was one of those who was in the group that killed Jon?"

"Yes. I feel the person, whoever's in prison, knows about what happened. And if I can get a lesser . . . 'cause I think they've got him in for all sorts of stuff. Some heavy . . . It'd be more felony than misdemeanor. And I felt slashing to my arms. I mean, God, that's a good clue, whoever that is. Unless there's some tattoos at the wrist area that people wear."

Noreen picked up Jon's shirt. She noticed a small paint mark on the chest area, and said, "I feel, ah . . . I'm nauseated. I feel confused. I . . . I feel very disoriented. I feel like I'm, I'm . . . Like, on . . . I don't know if something was given to me that drugged me . . . I feel like a rope might have hung me, but not necessarily in the place that I was found."

I asked, "How do we deal with these guys?"

"Cautiously," Noreen said. "These guys are talkers. These guys are braggers. They're also very frightened and scared to talk. So, it's sort of easier to cut them from the herd."

Noreen's literature had said she worked particularly well with metal objects, so I asked her to hold the metal D-ring on Jon's blue jeans.

"Yeah, there was something hooked on to here." Then, in a gruff voice, she added, "You don't think I'd just have things hanging onto my pants without a purpose."

I didn't hear her clearly and I said, "I didn't understand that."

"Ah, there's . . . sure . . . whole bunch of keys. I think only two were significant for the murderers. You're dealing with more than one person. It was a real good cover-up, because the cover-up involved, ah, a police person. You have a . . . Oh, God. It's . . ."

"Okay," I said. "I didn't want to say that before, but that's what we have suspected."

"Well, a police person," she said.

I didn't want to sidetrack her, so I asked her to continue. She hesitated and then seemed to be speaking directly to me.

"Oh, darn you," she said. "You know what's coming up now. You know I . . . what I'm seeing. And I feel more sheriff than police."

She asked if the sheriff had done the investigation, and I said the police had done it.

"Why do I see sheriff?" she asked herself. "I see a star, and my interpretation of the star, of course, was sheriff."

Jane asked, "Can you see people lifting him up onto that backstop?"

"Oh, absolutely. But I feel like I was dragged up there. I don't feel like I was killed there."

I asked if the police were directly involved in Jon's death, or if they simply came afterward and didn't follow up on it very well.

"I smell something," Noreen said. "I smell a rat. Might be a couple of them. I feel some, some bad . . . Oh, dear. I'm so sorry to say this. One is prominent, and there's more than one. And one is pretty powerful. And, so, it's like, oh, frantic people, frantic. Oh, this is . . ." She hesitated and then began speaking as if she was someone other than herself. "Look, we've got more important things to do."

"Important people?" I asked, having not clearly heard what she said.

"I feel some important people involved . . . but I don't know why they know . . . but they are . . . so, it had to be the drugs . . . or money laundering some way. What state are we?"

"Maryland."

"Maryland. Yeah. Probably drugs," she said.

I ran the names of a few police officers by her, and she gave me her impressions.

I asked about Victor Riemer.

"He scares me," Noreen said. "Victor scares me. Now, I don't know if he's a ferocious cop or just a scary bad . . . He scares me."

"Get any sense," I asked, "of involvement in Jon's death, as opposed to just being a bad guy?"

"He could just be a tough cop," Noreen said. "And if I was just the average person, then he would still scare me."

I had asked directly if Riemer was involved in Jon's death and, in her response, Ms. Renier had not said anything to indicate that he was. I noticed and moved on.

I gave her Chief of Police Robey's name.

"Sort of spit and polish," she said. "By the book."

I gave her the name of the previous chief of police.

"Chaney?"

"I get bad vibes with Chaney," she said.

By then, everyone involved was exhausted. We chatted a few minutes, said good-bye, and hung up.

Chapter Thirty-seven

WHEN THE PICTURE THE POLICE ARTIST DREW arrived in the mail, I took it to Sandra's. I laid it on her kitchen table and she picked it up and studied it.

"I have no idea who that is," she said.

She called Mickey and he came downstairs, looked at the picture, and said, "Nope. Nobody I know."

I typed a transcript of the reading and gave a copy to Rogers. He called me at work one afternoon after interviewing Brian Bumbrey, and he sounded out of breath.

"Noreen said the person we should talk to was continuing his education in prison. Right?"

"Right."

"Well, I walk in and Bumbrey's late for the appointment because he's studying for his high school equivalency test."

"I guess that's a fit."

"And you remember how she described some slashing or cutting on his wrists for pleasure, and then said that maybe it was a tattoo?"

"I remember."

"I never noticed it before, but on the underside of Bumbrey's forearm he has a large tattoo of a dagger."

"Damn," I said. "That's really getting close. Glasses?"

"He wears them when he studies."

"Southern accent?"

"Thick."

"Did he have anything new to add?"

"I was so blown away," Rogers said, "I could hardly think to ask him anything. He says he's still determined to see that justice is done in the Bowie case."

"Tattoo of a dagger, huh?"

"Plain as day. I thought I would pass out."

We passed around copies of the picture the police artist had drawn. No one recognized the person in the picture.

Sandra was convinced that we had to talk with Ms. Renier again. Although Ms. Renier's input had been illuminating and thought provoking, there was little we could follow up. The county police had already demonstrated that they had no interest in investigating the possibility that police officers were involved in drugs, and there was nothing concrete to give the FBI.

I took off work one afternoon in August and called Ms. Renier again, sitting at my kitchen table. I had a list of questions on the table in front of me, but Ms. Renier and her assistant had discussed the case before I called, and they wanted to summarize what they had covered.

Ms. Renier said that if I was facing the front of Sandra's house, I would go a certain number in one direction. She didn't know if the number was miles or feet or what it was. Then I would take two turns and go down the road a short distance. At that time, I would be standing in front of the killer's house, and I would be within a radius of just under three miles from Sandra's house. The killer's home was in an isolated location on a rural road, and she gave three numbers associated with it. She said I should consider all combinations of the numbers, which probably represented a mailbox number, but could be a street address or a road number.

The truck that was supposed to have picked up Jon after the party was American made and not too old. "Maybe 1989." It had been painted or it might be two-tone with different shades of the same color. You had to step up to get into the truck. She saw an orange and black sticker on the windshield, and a "strong bumper" in the front. "There's some chrome," she said. "Not a cheapo."

There were dozens of rural roads within a three-mile radius of the Keyser home. Throw in all possible combinations of the three mailbox, house, or maybe road numbers, and the task of finding a house or pickup truck that fit Ms. Renier's descriptions was a bit daunting.

But I tried, in my spare time after work and on weekends, completely without success.

I pieced together a scenario that involved some of Jon's friends. I was running this scenario by Sandra one evening at her kitchen table when she put her hands over her ears and sat up straight with a startled look on her face.

"I just heard Jon," she said. "He said, 'My friends wouldn't do this to me.'"

In March 1993, Noreen Renier called me at work and asked what had become of the case. I told her we were still holding on, but hadn't really made any progress.

"Maybe we should do it again," she said.

I couldn't commit without talking with Sandra, so I said I would have to get back to her. During lunch that day I drove across town to the daycare center and repeated the conversation to Sandra. I said I was willing but ambivalent. The fee was expensive, and I wasn't eager to chase around the county after more clues.

"Let's do it," Sandra said. "And this time, I want to be there."

On the day of the appointment we met at my house, and this time I used the upstairs extension and Sandra sat at my kitchen table and used the wall phone.

Ms. Renier described for the police artist what sounded like a completely different person who was at least partly responsible for Jon's death. He reminded her of a tough country person who, at that time, might have been called a Marlboro Man.

I had never liked how Officer Pete Wright kept appearing and disappearing in the assault charges against the police officers, and I asked if he could have done it.

Noreen paused a moment and said, "Pete doesn't have the guts."

Sandra asked if Ms. Renier could stand in front of the killer's house, and Ms. Renier saw an older house. The lawn was not well manicured, and there seemed to be engines around, which perhaps meant the person was mechanically inclined. She thought the house might be in the vicinity of where Sandra lived. She saw a small, old-fashioned church on the street, and the church might have been added onto or was near a newer church that had been built to replace it. This description included what looked to her like a nearby water tower, an interstate highway, some sort of major old tracks, and a large body of water. She gave me directions so I could draw clock positions on a map.

Noreen's assistant asked if Jon knew the murderer, and Noreen said, "I'm . . . I've known him. Everybody's known him and not known him. He's not a newcomer on the block. He's been here. Been almost, ah, convicted of another serious crime. Almost. Some technicality . . ."

Noreen's assistant asked for something significant about this person.

"Music," Noreen said. "Maybe there was something with music to . . . bound us, or bring us closer together. I think because he was so different, he attracted me. He seemed very free."

The atmosphere seemed to grow more intense, and Noreen said, "He hit me with a bat first. Hit me with something on my back first."

I asked, "Where are you when he hit you with the bat?"

"We weren't there. He had to drag or pull me there. It wasn't quite there. More toward the vehicles. That's where your witnesses were."

I asked, "How many people were there?"

"There's a bunch," Noreen said.

"And this is the place where you were hit with the bat?"

"This is the place that first there were some drugs. Ah, I feel some injection in me, maybe after I was hit."

"Where? Where do you feel it?" I asked.

"I can feel it . . . they're holding . . . I'm on the ground, or I'm down, and I feel just, ah, in my vein. In the elbow. I feel something going in me."

"When did you first know you were in trouble?"

"I knew I was in trouble at the party. I knew something was going on."

It wasn't clear to me if she meant that Jon knew that he was in trouble at the party where he had lost his keys, or if it had been afterward at some other gathering, so I asked if there had been another party.

"It was a party that was set up. I go to one party, and leave it at ten fifteen and we go someplace else, and that's where the trouble is. The trouble wasn't really all at the first party, but three of the people at the first party go on, and then there's more. Why? Why? I didn't do it. I didn't. I did. I really did. I—"

I would curse myself later for not asking what Jon really did or didn't do, but I was tired and I missed it at the time and only heard it later as I listened to the recording.

When the second picture arrived in the mail, it didn't look at all like the first. It really did resemble a rugged Marlboro Man. I took the picture to Sandra's and she looked at it and laid it on the table.

"No idea," she said. "Maybe it's two different people, and they're both involved."

I must have driven to, parked, and stared at every water tower in the county. There was a military base one county over, and there seemed to be a water tower at almost every intersection.

Ms. Renier had said there couldn't be that many old churches or churches being added onto in the area, but they were as plentiful as water towers. It was as if every congregation in the county had applied for a building permit.

Railroad tracks ran parallel to Interstate 95, and that seemed like the closest fit for the old tracks Noreen had said paralleled a major road, but there was also an old figure-eight race track, and the Laurel horse track, and numerous high school athletic tracks.

I found a house across the street from a high school that stood next to a water tower and had lots of old cars and trucks in the yard. It wasn't within the radius I was supposed to stay in, and the roads didn't run in the right directions to suit Ms. Renier's points in a circle. Still, I drove by every few days, as if I could look at it enough times and it would somehow become the right place.

I drew circles on paper and put the house we were looking for in the center, triangulated all that we knew, and searched, and searched.

Chapter Thirty-eight

I CALLED REVEREND ROGERS and asked him to talk with Brian Bumbrey one last time. I wanted Bumbrey to know that we were tired of all the tap dancing, that this had been going on long enough. I had already spoken with an attorney who agreed to serve as a go-between. If Bumbrey seemed mildly receptive, I asked Rogers to discuss a deal in which Bumbrey got a sentence reduction in exchange for full details that could be checked out.

"I can't do it," Rogers said.

"Why not?"

"I've already tried to talk to him again. There's a new policy at the prison. Ministers aren't allowed to talk to prisoners without special clearance. There's no way I could get clearance to talk to him."

I said, "Well, ain't that a surprise?"

Reverend Rogers called.

"I think I just did a bad thing," he said.

The Presbyterian Church, USA had a reputation for taking on important social issues, and Rogers had persuaded them to officially request that the Justice Department reopen the Bowie case. In a different matter, as part of some national committee he was on, Rogers was supposed to meet with representatives of the Justice Department. A woman named Linda Davis, who was the head of the Criminal Section of the Justice Department's Civil Rights Division, had called him about the upcoming meeting.

"I know that name," I said. "That's the person from the Justice Department who signed the letter to Sandra saying that the case was closed."

"Are you sure?" Rogers asked.

"Yes."

"Now I know I've done a bad thing," Rogers said. "I mentioned the Bowie case, and the request from the Presbyterian Church to reopen it. She said the Bowie case had been thoroughly investigated, and the request from the Presbyterian Church would be denied. "I went off," he said. "I mean, I really went off. I shouted at her for about five minutes. I shouted so long that, finally, when I calmed down, I felt that I had to apologize."

"This Linda Davis, how did she come across to you?"

"Professional, a bit of a bureaucrat, but intelligent. She said she would be willing to look at any new information about the Bowie case, but that it had already been thoroughly investigated."

"Then I have to disagree with you. I think you did a good thing."

"I don't understand."

"She said, in essence, that legitimate information could persuade her to reopen the case. What else would you want her to say?"

"I don't know," Rogers said. "I'm afraid I got pretty abusive."

"So what? She'll remember the Bowie case the next time it comes up."

"There's not much doubt about that," Rogers said.

It was early morning, and I was beginning to wake. The voice was very soft and yet perfectly clear. You could legitimately call it a still, small voice.

I knew from the words that the message was for Sandra, but I was running late and I didn't see how I could possibly stop by the daycare center before work. I worried that I had made it up, or that it had been part of a dream.

I developed a toothache that morning and called my dentist from the office, and he worked me in between other patients. He couldn't find anything wrong.

The dentist's office was near the daycare center where Sandra worked, and after the appointment I stopped by. Sandra was surprised to see me and had a puzzled look on her face when I asked if she could step outside for a moment. She told her assistant she would be right back, and we stepped outside toward the side of the building.

"Listen," I said. "I could be making this up, but I heard a voice, and there's something I need to tell you."

I could see by her dead calm that I had set her up to believe there was some source other than me, so I repeated my caution. "I'm serious," I said. "I mean, I heard the voice, but it could have been just a dream. The only reason I'm telling you is that I think it's something you need to hear, even if it's only me telling you."

"I understand," she said.

I told her it was long, and she would have to be patient and hear me out. Then I told her what I had heard:

"You know I love you like a sister, and I would never do anything to bring you harm or cause you pain, but you've been sad long enough."

She gripped my forearm and her eyes had a glazed and teary look, and she said, "Thank you."

"Wait," I said. "I told you it was long. There's more."

"When you are sad, you deny God's truth. You deny His joy and His will for your happiness. If you do it because you want Jon to know that you love him, he already knows that. If you do it to show that you care, caring is its own proof. You've been sad long enough."

"That's it," I said.

"Does your tooth still hurt?" she asked.

Forgetting that I had not mentioned my toothache, I said, "Not really. I'll take aspirin for a few days. I'm sure it'll be fine."

She thanked me again and added, "Interesting timing."

* * *

Sandra was new to meditation. She sat cross-legged with her back against a pillow, facing the foot of the bed and thinking how she never had a chance to tell Jon good-bye. She said a short prayer for guidance and protection and asked to be surrounded by light. The sound of footsteps coming up the stairs distracted her. She listened for a moment, annoyed at the interruption, and opened her eyes.

Jon stood at the foot of the bed, smiling. "I can't stay long," he said. "I came to say good-bye, because I know that's what you want. I also came to tell you something. You've been sad long enough."

He looked so real, but calmer, older, more mature, even taller. "You're a very handsome man," she said.

He came to the side of the bed, leaned over, and she felt his arms as he hugged her, his hand as he gave her back three solid pats, and his lips as he kissed her cheek. Then he was gone.

Sandra didn't think she could possibly sleep, but she pulled the covers out, crawled under, and slept soundly. The next morning, she woke and had been getting ready for work for as much as fifteen minutes before it came into her mind that, at last, Jon had visited her. Then, feeling a new sense of peace, all she could think was that he looked good. He looked really good.

By the time the Bowie-Keysers settled, the amount of Mickey's civil suit against the county had increased to six million dollars.

"It's not about the money," Sandra said. "It never was. What happened to Jon—and Mickey—shouldn't happen to anyone."

In their own ways, Mickey and Carlen got on with their lives. Mickey tried taking a prescription drug for depression, but it clouded his mind and he discontinued it after a couple of weeks.

Carlen was about to graduate from law school when she had a nervous breakdown. She sought counseling and came to realize that she had lived in denial of Jon's death, passionately throwing herself into studies, work, and parenting. She reassembled her life and succeeded admirably as a computer programmer. Both she and Mickey have commemorative tattoos honoring Jon.

There came a time when Mickey and Carlen realized that Jon had appeared to each of them in the same dream, and he said the same thing.

"Let it go."

I called Sandra from work one afternoon and said, "I think I know what happened."

"I just got a chill," she said. "What do you think happened?"

"I don't want to tell you yet. I want you to ask if I have it right."

"I'll try," she said.

She called back an hour or so later.

"Sometimes I use colors to help me," she said, "like green for yes and red for no. I asked if you had it right and all I could see was green. Then a red streak like lightning went down the center of the green, and I saw the words, 'Too dangerous.'"

I thought about that for a few moments. Then I told Sandra, "We have to drop it. It doesn't matter if I'm right or even close to right. We could get ourselves or someone else hurt, and that wouldn't accomplish anything that should be accomplished."

"Do you mean you're giving up?"

"Of course not," I said. "This is an important story. It needs to be told. I'm going to write it down before I forget."

On Christmas Eve, 1993, police were called to a trailer park just outside Columbia to deal with a domestic disturbance. A man named Melendez, who had a near-comatose blood alcohol level of .34, died at some point while being arrested and transported to the hospital. Melendez's nephew said a police officer kicked his uncle in the back of the head as he lay facedown and handcuffed on the living room floor. There was an investigation, a grand jury decided that no police officers had done anything wrong, and the man's family eventually sued the county for thirty-six million dollars.

Officer Riemer was one of the officers who responded to the call. A year later, just after Christmas 1994, Riemer's resignation from the Howard County police department was announced in passing about two-thirds of the way through a newspaper article about the Melendez case. A police source said in the article that Riemer's resignation had nothing to do with the Melendez case, or the Bowie case.

Sandra put two and two together and concluded that Riemer resigned from the police department the same day that Mickey graduated from college after the winter semester at the University of Maryland.

For months, on her eyelids, Sandra had seen a red barn surrounded by farm animals, and Confederate soldiers dressed in gray uniforms riding on horseback across spacious and rolling, grassy fields.

She had no idea what it meant.

Jim and Sandra finally found a new home in another state. They retired, and in July 1995 they rode away in Jim's still-spotless silver and burgundy van, leaving New America behind. There are lots of golf courses near where they moved. Sandra said before they left that Jim had earned it.

Occasionally, I took the long drive, and Jim and I played golf. I couldn't help noticing each time I approached their new home that I was passing red barns, surrounded by farm animals, near the spacious and rolling, grassy fields of a famous Civil War battlefield.

Acknowledgments

It is with great pleasure that I acknowledge the many people who helped with this book, and if I overlook some I should have remembered, please accept my sincerest apologies and appreciation.

They are:

Media producer Gracia Walker, who persuaded me that this was a task worth pursuing.

Rachel Cone-Gorham, who is so much more than a book agent. Her talent, skill, and diligence are the reason this book happened.

Michaela Hamilton, Editor in Chief, Citadel Press, who, in a stroke of genius, said I had to cut the manuscript significantly if I wanted Kensington to publish it.

Author, journalist, editor Lisa Pulitzer, who convinced me that there still was much to add, and showed me where and how.

Editor John Paine, who helped me improve the content by cutting it in half.

Patricia Cone for proofreading the manuscript the second or third time I mistakenly thought I was finished.

Longtime friend and retired English teacher Margaret Basinger, who generously offered her proofreading services when I really had all but finished, and her husband Dale Basinger, also a longtime friend, for his encouragement.

James Ferry, Columbia, MD, for the professional headshot.

Kensington CEO Steve Zacharius and the hardworking Kensington staff most closely associated with this project:

- Lynn Cully, publisher
- Vida Engstrand, head of marketing
- Darla Freeman, director of sales operations
- Michelle Addo, publicist
- Kristine Mills-Noble, creative director, and her design team

My wife, Jane, of course, and my sons, Mike and Dan, for their patience and honest critiques.

The Bowie-Keyser family—Jim, Sandra, Carlen, and Mickey—for sharing their lives and answering and re-answering my endless flood of questions.

The many people named in this book, and many more unnamed, who put their arms around this family and walked with them through this difficult journey—because that's what relatives, friends, neighbors, and sometimes even strangers, so often do.